Chānakya

Rules of Governance by the Guru of Governance

Chānakya is known for
*Destroying and Creating
Demolishing and Establishing
Uprooting and Planting
Over-ruling and Framing Rules
Disturbing and Managing
Displacing and Governing*

**Learn the Art, Science and Tactics
As Given in the Kautilya Arthashāstra.**

Prof. Shrikant Prasoon

V&S PUBLISHERS

Published by:

V&S PUBLISHERS

F-2/16, Ansari Road, Daryaganj, New Delhi-110002
23240026, 23240027 • *Fax:* 011-23240028
Email: info@vspublishers.com

Branch : Hyderabad
5-1-707/1, Brij Bhawan (Beside Central Bank of India Lane)
Bank Street, Koti, Hyderabad - 500 095
040-24737290
E-mail: vspublishershyd@gmail.com

Follow us on:

All books available at **www.vspublishers.com**

© **Copyright:** *V&S* **PUBLISHERS**
ISBN 978-93-814489-8-4
Edition: 2012

Printed at: Param Offseters, Okhla, New Delhi-110020

Dedication

Dedicated to All
Who Wish and Try to Manage:
Self; Family; Society
And their Organization
For Greater Gain
And Higher Attainment

Contents

Section I
Life and Sutra

Section II
Kautilya Arthshastra

Section III
Conclusion and Niti Shastra

Preface

Chānakya thought on all related branches and boughs of management keeping a really big empire at the centre for focus. He thought for all; for the benefit, survival and prosperity of all; so this book is for all: Writers, Thinkers, Managers, Politicians, Human Resource Personnel, Military Personnel, Traders, Management Trainers, Management Consultants, Management Trainees, Management Students, Government Officials and General Readers.

In this book I have tried to write Chānakya's biography; his achievements and accomplishments and his ideas about accumulating wealth, establishing, managing and ruling an empire. I have done the best that was possible.

Now, it is up you, the readers, to judge whether I have been able to present and reveal the real Chānakya or not; whether his relation with management is established well or not; whether ancient management is described in detail with reference to modern management or not, and whether I have given everything that you need for growth and prosperity or not. It will be a real pleasure if the readers get a lot more than their expectation.

Only "ā" has been taken from scriptural Transliteration for the long "a" sound, which is otherwise impossible to write in the Roman script. Rest everything is as written in government papers, magazines, newspapers and general books. It will help the readers read the few Mantras and many *Sutras* and Shlokas quoted in it.

Sarve Shubhe!

Prof. Shrikant Prasoon

Prayers

Prayers by Chãnakya

Pranamya shirsā Vishnum trailokyādhipatim prabhum
Nānāshāstroddhritam wakshye rājnitisamuchayam.

After humbly bowing down to the Emperor of the three worlds (the Earth, Heaven and Hell) the Almighty Bhagawān Vishnu, I herewith present the maxims of the science of political ethics, i.e. *Rajnitishāstra*, selected from different treaties/scriptures.

❖❖❖

Adhityedam yathāshāstram naro jānāti sattamah
Dharmopadeshvikhyātam kāryākāryam subhāsubham.

By studying these maxims taken from the shātras one acquires knowledge of the best principles to be followed in life and understands what ought or what ought not to be done, what is good or bad, religious or non-religious, sin or virtue.

❖❖❖

Tadaham sampravakshyāmi lokānām hitakāmyayā
Yen vugyānmātrena sarbagyatwam prapadyate.

Therefore with an eye to the public good, I'm presenting that knowledge which will lead to the correct understanding of things in their proper perspective, if and when learnt well.

❖❖❖

Namãmi

Abhayam mitrād- abhayam- amitrad- abhayam gyātād-abhayam puro yeh,
Abhayam naktam-abhayam diwā nah sarvā āshā mama mitram bhawantu.

Atharva Veda 19:15:6

अभयं मित्रदभयममित्रदभयं ज्ञातादभयं पुरो य: ।
अभयं नद्रमभयं दिवा न: सर्वा आज्ञा मम मित्रं भवन्तु ।

O God! We should not be afraid of friends or enemies;
make us free from fear of known persons and all other things;
we should be fearless during day and night; there should not
be any cause of any fear in any country; and everywhere
we get friends, and only friends.

❖❖❖

Bhadram no api wātaya mano dakshamuta kratum.

(Rigveda 10:25:1)

भद्रं नो अपि वातय मनो दक्षमुत क्रतुम् ।

O God! Give us liberal heart, generous work
and bountiful strength.

❖❖❖

Vaishwānar- jyotih- bhuyāsam.

(Yajurveda 20:23)

वैवानरज्योतिर्भूयासम् ।

O God! Make me absorb your bountiful light.

Chānakya in Spiritual Quadruplets

◄ 1 ►

The original management Guru Chānakya thought of organized self cardinal;
Of managing family well, maintaining relations and improving social set up;
Raising and developing organizations and administration of a big–small empire.
His useful and pragmatic views made both the ideas and person immortal.

◄ 2 ►

The son of Rishi Chanak, Chānakya was Takshasheelā's meritorious product;
A keen observer who analyzed, synthesized, was able to induct and deduct;
Capable of clearing the hurdles heavy and uprooting obstructions outrightly:
Knew to abduct the desired and undesired obliterate, obstruct or defunct.

◄ 3 ►

Chānakya was made up of opposing elements; crude–smooth, kind–cruel;
Attached to promises, detached from gains, extinguishing, flaming fuel;
Without being cruel or curved or with utmost cruelty and deep sweetness;
He created one policy for each thing in non-committed manners dual.

◄ 4 ►

He raised an alert army equipped with arms and expert fighters youthful;
Working throughout the days, active and busy throughout the nights, fateful;
He created from straw a crown golden, jewelled, bright, large and majestic.
Won consistently in piecemeal for a pupil brilliant, obedient and truthful;

◄ 5 ►

The person with thin body when needed roared like an awesome thunder;
He planned a full proof system systematically; it is the greatest wonder;
Made paths, carts, wheels, and made them run on smoothly, rhythmically:
Obstacle free forward, for he allowed none to commit a mistake or blunder.

The creative thinker in him vehemently criticized each ill and deformity;
He wanted to, acted for, forced for behaviour and actions to be in conformity;
Filled up with intellectual power, balanced reasoning, reached a conclusion:
With humble submission to the Almighty, he possessed spiritual sublimity.

He tirelessly and intelligently worked to create one powerful nation;
By bringing small kingdoms under it or usurping with pious intention;
By ousting attackers; finishing weak, with treaties and key marriages:
By strengthening army, changing administration, like an expert mason.

He appointed performing executives and opponent as Amātya, the Chief;
And relinquished the coveted post for arranging ideas immortal and stiff;
He performed with meticulous precision and with overwhelming success:
With a tranquil mind and in the self with utmost confidence and belief.

Chānakya provoked and was provoked to take a true candid vow;
He diligently scripted new golden bright chapters many in a row;
He performed with spiritual insight and benign worldly wisdom:
During his time he was a great showman and an enchanting show.

He was a realist, idealist and a pagan; magnanimous, lenient and brute;
He was a racist, fascist and also mystic, a root, stem, branch and soot;
A mind master, a servant and one who generated services ample:
Above all, a perennial fragrant flower and rejuvenated energized fruit;

First he himself followed then he gave wise lessons to the posterity;
They are prized, cherished, illuminating, immense fully free property;
Experienced statesman and learned Āchārya wrote dictums-aphorisms:
The teachings are enough for health, happiness, peace and prosperity.

No praise, eulogy or obeisance will be enough for soft metallic man;
Who knew and was friendly with Time which always after him ran:
When deeds glowed, success followed, victory garlanded, fame spread:
So, imbibe, imitate, absorb him in total, and be like Chānakya if you can.

From Spiritual Quadruplets

Life and Sutra

DRIDHA-PRATIGYA VIJAYI
DETERMINED VICTOR

Chānakya:
Man, Life and Governance

There are certain super conscious human beings, positive and creative thinkers who acquire immense power of knowledge and wisdom that in reality they change the course of time and history of the period. They are so effective that history takes the course that they dictate. Without any doubt Chānakya was such a legendary figure. No other human being of the past or present can claim to be closer to Chānakya in knowledge, wisdom, practical approach, character, integrity and performance. The most wonderful thing is that he lived like a saint, accumulated nothing other than knowledge and fame for himself. He did everything for others, for the betterment of the life of the people, for the betterment of society, and the security of the country.

Chānakya is symbolised by *Dhoti* as *adho vastram* and a folded shawl on the shoulders as *angvastram*; open plait at the back of large, shining head with big bright eyes, wide and glowing forehead and black colour; books in hand as knowledge in possession. Such was Chānakya, the brilliant, determined and wise *ācharya* and son of Rishi Channak.

People like Chānakya continue to live through the centuries through their teachings. People die but their words and ideas are passed on by men of the coming generations. It is essential and valuable for them and the posterity, for the future of human beings. Chānakya is living and an active thinking and guiding force as ideas.

Chānakya: A Fair Administrator

Chānakya was an esteemed thinker and man of quick and lasting action; a strict teacher and fair administrator; an immaculate strategist and manipulator; a dexterous planner and extraordinary executive; a destructive force and creative energy; rational and highly emotional; an annihilator of a kingdom and creator of a dynasty; he was always superb and performed very close to perfection. He did everything with his mental power. He was an *āchārya* and had been teaching at the university for a few years when he took up the vow to demolish the Nand dynasty. He had left the profession of teaching to share his wisdom and do good with the society. The Nand dynasty was either sucking the people dry or throwing them into luxury and unscrupulous works. It spelt disaster for the society and the country. Chānakya demolished it with character and grace. He had no money, no power, no post and no army, yet with his mental agility and determined effort he created an emperor out of a village child, raised a big, capable and well-furnished army and accomplished an impossible task. He realized the power of wisdom. He was also an exemplary writer who declared: *buddhiryasya balam tasya nirbuddhestu kuto balam,* which means, "only he is powerful who has wisdom."

That single and simple event changed the history of India, that single Brahmin has changed the life and attitude of the millions of men in every century down the ages. With his own effort he has become a high mountain which can't be scaled; a deep sea which can't be fathomed; a blowing wind which can't be checked and the purest human being who can't be won. Chānakya is bigger than a shāl tree, fertile as a basin, secure as a cave and illuminating as rays. He is worshipped and feared at the same time. It's the living force of that man who worked and inspired countless volcanic transformers some 2,500 years ago and still continues to inspire numerous souls for greater achievements.

Personal Expenses Vs Treasury Expenses

One incident is enough to throw ample light on the nature, character, behaviour, sincerity and honesty of Chānakya – a superb and dominating figure of all times.

This incident of changing the lamp before allowing the visitor to sit and before entering into a conversation has been described by Megasthanese in India. It is related to him. He had come to India and had heard about Chānakya. He wanted to meet him. It was not difficult to meet him. He sent a message and was allowed to go to the hut in which Chānakya was living.

When Megasthanese went there, it was the first hour of the evening. Chānakya was writing something under the dim light of an earthen lamp. He raised his head, welcomed the guest and asked politely, "What's your purpose?"

"I've come to see you and talk to you about yourself and on different topics." It was the candid reply of the foreigner.

Chānakya asked him to wait. Then he took another lamp and after lighting it he put off the first lamp. Then he invited Megasthanese to sit on a broad mat. He sat down but he could not hide his surprise. He asked,

"I feel there must be a reason that you have put off the first lamp and lighted another one but I don't find any difference between them; neither in the shape and size nor the light that it is emitting. Please tell me why did you change the lamp?"

Chānakya gave a simple reply. "Before changing the lamp I asked about your

purpose. I came to know that this is a personal meeting. So I put off the official lamp whose oil comes from the government treasury and I lighted the lamp for which I purchase oil from my salary. While doing a personal work I can't misuse the government's money."

The visitor did not know how to react. He knew Chānakya was all powerful in the Maurya kingdom yet he was behaving in such an honest way. He bowed before him and said,

"This is the reason of your immense power."

Appraisal

Transfer of fund from one head or project to another is dangerous. It creates misunderstanding in internal relationship and hazards in the completion of the projects. In place of transferring the fund, genuine efforts must be made to raise separate fund for each work and project.

Effect

Mix the money, mind and work; effort will get mixed. Any mix is fatal for every organization.

2

A Creative Thinker

Chānakya was a creative thinker, a famous intellectual, a tireless worker, an imaginative organizer, a detached minister, a determined fighter, a performing executive, a controlling economist, a secret adviser, a meticulous planner, a mysterious protagonist, and an experienced statesman. In all that, he had no peer. It is an accepted fact that in his absence his books are doing what he was able to do. This way, his strength has become the creative and managing power for millions.

Chānakya, the first, original and victorius management guru, is treated as the first Economist; the first one to theorize administration and management. He is a living, active and immortal teacher, writer and statesman. He destroyed the ruling Nand dynasty and established a bigger and stronger Maurya dynasty.

Chānakya was the greatest and most powerful thinker, minister, organizer, and director, known in the history so far. His actual greatness lies in the fact that he relinquished the post of the Prime Minister, at the peak of his career, after establishing the biggest and greatest empire in India by bringing it under one rule and changing it into a "United Whole". He retired for writing books and teaching and training other administrators; he actually did it to be free from daily administrative rituals and thus to be able to keep an eye over everything for strengthening the king, kingdom, and administration.

A very tough administrator, Chānakya collected the existing laws and regulations and on that basis created his own rules for petty things like weight and measure to the great and successful strategy for attack and defense.

Management Wizard

Kautilya, who was widely known as Chānakya, was the world's first management guru. His management thoughts and ideas helped kings and rulers for centuries. Chānakya himself first practised it as a test case through his disciple Chandragupta, a village lad whom he first made the king of Magadha after demolishing the reign of the Nand dynasty and then expanded it and covered the extreme borders. All neighbouring kingdoms came under his rule, the rule of the Maurya dynasty. It is known as Brihattar Bhārata, greater India.

All the powerful kings in ancient India like Ashoka had learnt the *Arthashāstra* and practised it to expand their kingdom multifold. How do the kings and rulers of today's corporate world apply his techniques in their respective organizations?

No wonder scholars down the centuries have time and again described Chānakya as a mastermind who could be an expert in so many varied and specialized fields.

He was responsible for bringing down the Nand dynasty and establishing his able student Chandragupta Maurya on the throne as the emperor. This is the reason why he is called a "Maker of Kings". He is also credited with having masterminded the defeat of Alexander the Great in India, when he was on the path to conquer the world.

As a political thinker, he was the first in history to visualize the concept of a Nation. During his time, India was split into various kingdoms. He brought all of them together, under one central governance, thus reuniting the oldest nation called Aryāvarta. It was also known as *Bhārat Varsha*. It is now known as Bhārat, Hindustan or India.

Chānakya was one of the great men and legendary characters in history who shaped time through their vision and exemplary actions; Chānakya, perhaps, is the only personality who has been accepted and revered as a genius both by Indian and Western scholars. He is a historical milestone in the making of India amidst tremendous upheavals and myriad's of reversals. Celebrated as a shrewd statesman and a ruthless administrator, he comes across as one of the greatest diplomats of the world. He had the guts to speak his heart out even in front of the rulers, which shows his strong inclination towards democratic values and the audacity to put his views across. Although he lived around the 3rd century BC, his ideas and principles show concurrence and validity in the present day world. Politics was his forte. Diplomacy in a politically-charged environment shows his self-confidence and the ability to stay calm in trying situations.

His foresight and wide knowledge coupled with politics of expediency founded the mighty Mauryan Empire in India. He was a great laureate of economics with a glittering intellect to perceive the intricate dynamics of various economic activities and principles.

Written Works

Chānakya, apart from being a man of wisdom and unfailing strategies, propounded Nitishāstra, the ideal way of living for every individual of the society. He looked at the country like a person surrounded by problems. He worked at the total annihilation of problems from the roots. The re-appearance of troubles only shows its growth. His contribution to foreign policy in the present day world is immense. Universities teach his principles to aspiring foreign policy experts showing the infallability of his principles. Chānakya's art of diplomacy is well known across India and practised in the areas of defence, strategy formation, and foreign relations.

What the Western thinkers repeated in 20th century that "War is only the continuance of state policy by other means",

Chānakya had already written it in his book *Chānakyaniti.* Most of his views were so farsighted that they appeared to be prophecies. Talking on diverse subjects such as corruption, he commented very rightly, "It's just as difficult to detect an official's dishonesty as it is to discover how much water the swimming fish drink." Most of these views and some new ones are contained also in his book *Vriddha Chānakya.*

He documented his life-long work in his book *Arthashāstra.* For ages, rulers across the world have referred to the *Arthashāstra* for building a nation on sound economics, based on spiritual values. Emperor Ashoka is supposed to have built and expanded his kingdom on the principles described in this book. Shivāji, the ruler of the Indian state of Maharashtra, is said to have studied this book in order to plan and defeat the Mughals.

As a person, Chānakya has been described in many ways be it as a saint, as a "ruthless administrator", as the "maker of kings", a devoted nationalist, a selfless ascetic it, and a person devoid of all morals. He created controversy by saying, "The ends justify the means" and the ruler should use any means to attain his goals and his actions required no moral sanctions. His great work *Arthashāstra* shows him in a different light and perspective.

Subjects Taught at Takshasheelā

A lot is not known about Chānakya's childhood and education, but he completed his education at *Takshasheelā (also Taxila)* where it was the tradition to teach *Sāhitya,* language and literature first, then *Dharma Shāstra,* scriptures, and then other *Shāstras* under the combined heading of *Darshan* which was usually called *Sāhitya aur Darshan.* His achievements, his books and his wide knowledge, deep concept, and apt and appropriate expression are proof that he must have been *Prgyā vāna,* the learned person who knew the past, present and future. He was not simply *Buddhimān* who sees only the present, nor *Matimān* who sees only the past. He knew *Trikāla,* all the three divisions of time.

Chānakya was educated at Taksheelā which boasts to be the greatest International University. Students were first taught all the subjects available there and then they opted for specialization. Chānakya also did that and gained mastery over many subjects.

Takshashila was Chānakya's breeding ground for acquiring knowledge in the practical and theoretical aspects. The teachers were highly knowledgeable who used to teach the sons of kings. The branches of studies most sought after in and around India ranged from law, medicine, warfare, and other indigenous forms of learning. The four Vedas, i.e., archery, hunting, elephant-lore, and the eighteen arts were taught at the University of Takshasheelā. The list does not show botany, animal husbandry, herbs and poisons, etc. He had mastery over them too. Either these subjects were topics allied to others or he learnt them from somewhere else.

The subjects taught in the University of Tākshasheelā were:

➢ Science
➢ Philosophy
➢ Āmmar of various languages
➢ Mathematics
➢ Economics
➢ Astrology
➢ Geography

➢ Astronomy
➢ Surgical science
➢ Agricultural sciences
➢ Archery
➢ Ancient science
➢ Modern sciences

The university also used to conduct researches on various subjects. From there on, specialization started. Otherwise all the students were taught all the subjects, so that, when they passed out, they had a lot in them: power of wisdom and mental agility.

Chānakya Comes to Pātaliputra

Though Chānakya was just a professor at the Takshasheelā University, which seemed to be far away from the happenings the country, he actually was able to influence the governments in a biger way. His students looked at him as an ideal teacher who inspired and exemplified great knowledge. His students respected him and were ready to fight at any moment at his orders. Two of his students, Bhadradatt and Purushdatt, have been mentioned at various places, and they played a pivotal role as his chief assistants.

There are different tales told to be the basis of dispute between Mahānand and Chānakya. The only certain thing is that hurt and angry Chānakya loosened his ritualistic plait at the centre of head and took a vow to destroy the Nand dynasty, him and his posterity. He promised not to bind the loosened plait till then, which constantly reminded him every now and then of the vow he had taken.

Before defeating the Nands, Chānakya had to employ various strategies for victory. Chānakya first tested the policy of attacking the core of the city. The policy met with defeats again and again. With the change in strategy, Chānakya and Chandragupta began the attack on the borders of the Magadha Empire. Chānakya envisioned India as a nation which would place itself as the forerunner – politically, economically, and socially.

Aims: Four Pursuits

The momentous life of Chānakya reminds us of some of his sayings that moulded his life and mind.

"The secret task of a king is to strive for the welfare of his people incessantly. The administration of the kingdom is his religious duty. His greatest gift would be to treat all as equals."

"The happiness of the commoners is the happiness of the king. Their welfare is his welfare. A king should never think of his personal interest or welfare, but should try to find his joy in the joy of his subjects."

After putting Chandragupta on the throne and making Mudrā Rākshasā as the Amātya, Chānakya devoted himself towards making the governance and the life of the people better. He truly followed the four pursuits of human life: *Dharma, Artha, Kāma* and *Moksha*.

He knew his *Dharma*, i.e., the righteous and moral deeds which he performed with all intensity, intelligence, ability, and spiritual intent.

Kāma was work, only work for him: incessant and diligently. He remained active till the end.

Artha was needed only for living, not in cash but in kind, utility goods which he got in abundance and felt no scarcity of. He lived such a simple life that money became meaningless for him. It is a wonder that the person, who preached wealth and inspired others to be wealthy, had no wealth and actually, no need for wealth. He created treasure, but for others.

For *Moksha*, he stopped taking his meals. He sat on a mound of manure, for free electrical flow, for absorbing as much cosmic energy as possible. This way, he forced his own death to materialize. He got *Moksha*, so he is a spirit now, a powerful spirit who adds values and power to an individual's spirit.

Multifaceted Personality

From nowhere to everywhere and from nothing to everything is the history of Chānakya's ascent to everlasting world fame. It was possible only because he was an imaginative organizer who visualized the problems ahead and solved them before they could raise their head and create obstacles.

Chānakya proved to be a detached minister as it was not his ultimate aim. He had taken all such responsibilities because he had to demolish the Nand dynasty, otherwise he was just a scholar and scholars in India have never shown lust, particularly lust for power and riches. So, when the Maurya dynasty was safe and secure, he forcibly handed over the post and charge to Nand's Amātya, Mudrā Rākshasā and took voluntary retirement for writing books.

The very fact that he took a vow and worked for years to make the vow come true shows clearly that Chānkya was a determined fighter. There are many examples of determination but Chānakya sustained that determination throughout his life and this is something strange and unique and cannot easily be found anywhere else.

Chānakya was not a minister who placed his initials simply on the files that came to him for signature. He needed no files. He was a meticulous planner. He planned, started, initiated and wrote the files, signed, passed the letters, and saw that the dictates are followed to the letter. He was not an idle onlooker but a performing executive, active right in the middle of all actions and controlling and balancing each of them by moving or even without moving towards it.

One need not search examples where Chānakya was a controlling economist. He created resources and accumulated wealth and spent it wisely on all and for various purposes at different places and under different heads, yet the closing balance was enough to last for decades to come.

Chānakya was definitely a mysterious protagonist and experienced statesman whose life and deeds are surrounded with mystery. His experiences were self-created and self collected. He had the theoretical knowledge and on that strong basis he imagined the problems and thought out solutions and implemented everything with greater ease and enormous success.

He advised himself more, less to the king, little to others and proved to be a secret adviser during his lifetime, but before he died he wrote down everything for everyone and became a universal adviser and the first and original management guru, the real Āchārya with his great treaties.

Tough Nature and Selfless Deeds

Chānakya is not a person who can please others. He is a very tough customer. Life is not easy and one should never wish or try to lead an easy life. Life is the greatest challenge. Every moment of it should be utilized for betterment, growth, perfection and salvation. Such purification of human nature and selfless deeds are essential. Naturally, he was all out for wisdom, purification, action, dutifulness and righteousness.

Sleepless Endeavour

A few villagers had gathered, mostly washermen, fishermen, and gardeners and were going towards their fixed destinations for washing clothes or catching fish or gathering flowers. They were standing, smiling and enjoying the sight in Āchārya Chānakya's open school in a very large mango orchard almost at the end of the villages and beginning of the lake.

First they wondered why the Guru was bringing two pitchers full of water towards the sleeping pupils. It was not the custom. The teacher was not allowed to do menial jobs. The pupils used to do that.

But then something strange happened and they all laughed. The Guru started pouring water from the pitcher on to the sleeping pupils. They woke up and without waiting even to tidy their clothes ran towards the lake. They ran helter-skelter and then ran ahead without looking back. They were confused and in a hurry, which provided entertainment to the men watching them.

They heard the teacher's angry words. All of them woke up because of the unexpected commotion and the sound of the teacher. There was no water in the first pitcher. He placed it down and went to take the other pitcher. He picked it up and turned towards the pupils. He found none there. They all had gone towards the lake.

He placed the pitcher at its place and went up to his seat and sat down. The villagers returned. The drama was over. Praising the teacher, the few workmen went on to perform their duties.

Appraisal

Incessant and tireless effort brings success even to those who are neither well-equipped nor strong enough. Regularity at work makes the difference. By incessant rubbing even soft rope makes its mark on hard stone.

Effect

One can increase one's day and working hours by rising early in the morning and returning to bed late at night, getting adequate sleep of six or seven hours from 10 PM to 5 AM. Those who go to bed very late, rise late and are not fresh.

Sublimity or Degeneration

Chānakya generates fear. He creates awe. He hurls a teacher's long thin stick which strikes hard and the ensuing pain lasts. In the present scenario when the corrupts are the powerful, when virtually there is no punishment for crimes and in numerous cases the criminals and degenerated people are honoured and venerated, a Chānakya is needed to overhaul the system, to deal sternly with the people and problems, to give severe punishment to the accused to bring changes for a better society and kingdom to live in. In one *sutra* he has mentioned that one should not live in a kingdom where there is terror: *Anupadrawam deshamā*. The world is in the grip of terror. There is no place worth living in the world. There is not a single country which has peace and there is no single profession which is not corrupt. All are selfish and ready to commit any type of crime for personal gain while Chānakya taught us to sacrifice one's interest when the interest of the society or the country is at stake: *janapadār tham grāmam tyajet* and *grāmārtham kutumbastyajet*. No one will be ready today to follow his teachings though modern man will lead a painful life and face the problems mostly created by wives and children; brothers and friends; because there is actually no check on immoral act and degeneration of the once sublime human life which is fast turning into animal world.

On the contrary to the fear that he generated, Chānakya taught fearlessness. He treated it to be a virtue, for fearlessness comes out of purity, honesty, sincerity and such other qualities. Whenever a door opens a criminal imagines the arrival of the police. He has no peace. In such a condition all the means of pleasure and luxury become meaningless. Chānakya advocated a fearless life which comes the hard way. The worst are not afraid of the insults; the wise and conscious are not afraid of employment or profession; they are not afraid of falls who have control over their senses; and those who have been honest and dutiful are not afraid of death:

(i) Nāstya mānabhayam anāryasya
(ii) Na chetanwattām britibhayam
(iii) Na jeetendriyānām vishayabhayam
(iv) Na kritārthānām maranbhayam

That fearless individual is one man in the known history that steadily grew and ascended up and up on the vertical ladder of wisdom, action, fame and respect, and never stepped down.

Protected Religion

Dharma was the most important thing for Chānakya. Dharma signifies "righteousness and one's duty towards self, family, society, the earth and the universal order." Artha follows Dharma but in the Indian context it has a much wider significance than merely 'wealth' as envisaged by the West. It's not only the maintenance of the law and order and administrative machinery that is important; in fact the maintenance of the self, the body, its machinery and family and social order is also important. Chānakya saw and felt all and tried his best to make others see and feel them. Here lies his unparalleled success and greatness. He did nothing for the selfish self; he did everything for the selfless self. He ensured the protection of the king, security to the kingdom and safety and prosperity to the people. He had a great inclination for democratic values.

Chānakya is an immortal genius even though he lived in Chānaki Garh in Champakāranya. His fame and activities and influence are still growing in all the four directions. He had a pure heart and a clean mind and saved the Dharma, in return the Dharma saved him: *Dharmo rakshati rakshitah*.

There are various facets and phases in the life of Chānakya in which "known wisdom and imperceptible execution" are at the top though he faced many reversals and upheavals. It's difficult for anyone to match a facet or a phase, a side or an angle which are so sharp and bright. Even many combined together can't match Chānakya. Thus it's obvious that Chānakya is incomparable. He has many names and should have more names. In fact, expert statesman, wise sage (ascetic), nationalist, ruthless administrator, maker of kings, and many more, are all his names. He had various qualities such as wisdom, courage, confidence, diplomacy, calmness, fearlessness, perseverance, and many more.

Chānakya is among the easiest to understand and very difficult to follow. If "sandhi", which can be called "synapse" (if a term from medical science is applied to grammar) is separated and the words are written separately then he would prove to be the simplest writer on the most general and intricate subjects and problems.

He is considered to be "angry, prejudiced, and stubborn". He had a solid and profitable reason behind being so and showed them in such a way, at such moments, and for such causes that he gains a lot from his anger, prejudice and stubbornness. It's also rare among the rarest in human history. All these traits in a human being are enough to ruin him; Chānakya thrived with them because he was not selfish and he never thought of or preferred selfishness.

He is simultaneously a practical man of the soil and with unheard of successes he became an idea, a percept and a philosophy; he didn't remain simply a man.

Chānakya must be intently and thoroughly read and his teachings must be rigorously, boldly, painfully, and sincerely followed for better vision, sure success, and greater gain.

To establish all these facts, one or two examples will be enough. One may read the 19th *Adhyāyya* of 15th *Prakarana* of 1st *Adhikaran* entitled: *Nishant Pranidhih*; and the 20th *Adhyāya* "*Ātma Rakshitakam*". What a grand arrangement he has suggested for the king's residence! What great precautions for its safety! What employees for menial works in inner and outer houses! What simple ways to recognize the dangerous agents! What a great warning! After giving all these he warns the king that as a king uses every method to bring harm to another king, in the same manner a king should take all precautions to save self, family, employees and citizens from those ways adopted by enemies:

Yathā cha yoga purushaih anya rājā apratishthati;
Tathā yayam anya bādhebhyo rakshed ātmānam ātmavān.

Chānakya was an illustrious scholar beaming with wisdom enriched by fresh knowledge that covered the widest range and included *Dharma Shāstra*, the scriptures; *Sāhitya*, language and Literature; *Darshan*, philosophy; *Chhand*, figures of speech and metres; *Vyākaran*, grammar; *Ashtra Vidyā*, weaponry; *Jyotisha*, astrology and astronomy; and *Āyurveda*, medicine. His knowledge was deep, varied and covered a wide range which cannot be imagined by a person in modern age that lays undue stress on a particular part of a branch of knowledge.

Chānakya was a balanced man standing at the centre far away from this extreme and that extreme. Often when he talked of rigorous punishment, mostly capital punishment, then it gives the illusion that he too is an extremist but no, he thought that the best way to control crime is capital punishment. The whole world is suffering from rampant crime because there is almost no punishment, if there is, then it is meager, and it rouses a feeling that the people are afraid of the criminals and hence not punishing them adequately. The fear is that of the attacks on them and their families. But Chānakya was fearless so he thought correctly and concluded rightly. This added a balancing factor to his inner self and turned him into a creative thinker.

The more the world sees this reputed intellectual the more fascinated they are. A single person can absorb so much power in his tiny brain, so many ideas, teaching lessons and work orders and can use them simultaneously with ease and dexterity.

Difficult Vow Accomplished

Chānakya had taken such a difficult and rare vow that he was not able to live at ease and take adequate rest and enjoy needed leisure. He had to arrange each and everything, from a simple needle to a sharp and heavy sword. This made him a tireless worker busy almost the whole day and whole night and in-between taking a nap here and an hour's sleep there. It is clear that he has been described working early in the morning, late in evening and even after midnight. In modern times many get night duty but they compensate the loss of sleep during the day. Yet they fell ill. What an inner strength Chānakya possessed!

It is better to die than preserve life by incurring disgrace. The loss of life only pains a moment, but disgrace, every day of one's life.

Chānakya had no peer; neither in totality of integrated knowledge nor in a particular field. There is none to measure his height or to dive deep to the bottom of his depth. The more one reads and thinks, the more one feels bewildered at the length and width that his writing covers. Even now, there is no other single book that covers so many important topics related to life, its rule, the ruler, the subject, the crime, the punishment or can compete with the *Arthashāstra* in range and details. The subtle divisions that he made of different things is a revelation; for example the division of *Guptachars* or *lābha*, income or profit, is brilliant. From the social and personal to sublime and divine height that he takes and soars up with his moral teaching in the *Niti Shāstra* can't be matched by even a collection composed by many *Nitigya*. The aphorisms that he has created with four to eight words are so condensed and so deep in meaning that they can't be fathomed by any. They can't even be compared to any other author as there is no wise pandit in any language of the world who has given such true and condensed sayings. Chānakya was unparalleled.

Chānakya showed how to ensure that a vow comes true by uprooting the strong Nand dynasty, the ruler of the Magadha Empire with all its roots and soot, stems and branches. It became traceless. It was a grand success for a stranger in the region who was alone and without familiar faces and companions. It is the only example of a strong empire being uprooted by an unestablished fresher from a University who had neither wealth nor army; neither a house nor a living; neither land nor residence; neither known people nor known resources; and neither weapons nor physical strength. That is why he declares that knowledge and wisdom is everything, the only success mantra.

Chānakya worked with so much of patience, and with such skill and swiftness that the others were busy in deciphering and understanding the first move but faced many more moves. He did not wait for the opposition to retaliate. He had time, but he gave no time, no space and no opportunity to others. That was the reason that he collected many in no time, ordered many regularly, accumulated wealth, weapon and youth with zeal and stamina. It was the sole reason that no ruin of the Magadh Empire came to light, it was such a smooth transfer that the people could not feel the gap because Chānakya built up a strong empire bit by bit replacing everything existing with fresh, strong and durable ones. He had substitute ready for each part, person and place of the debris of the uprooted empire. There was a complete over whiling but it was not felt by the people as there were no substantial disturbances to them.

In an amazing fashion Chānakya brought a big and varied country like India under one rule. He applied all the methods that he has dictated in his immortal books, luring some, creating fear in some, entering into treaty with many, fighting battles and defeating the rigid ones but he brought them together and united the whole country that included many foreign lands of the modern world. During his time they were integral parts of Brihattar Bhārat, Greater India.

Organized Whole

Chānakya was a well-organized person. The ideas came to him in a planned sequence. So he was able to make synchronized moves at different places and of different nature simultaneously. With personal example, he showed the world how everything can be managed: from self to big organizations; from a small group of inexperienced fighters to a national army of multi caste, creed, faith and opinion.

It may be debatable whether he was "perfect" or not as no one is perfect; but with his theories and practise, he comes really close to perfection. One can see a part of him or many parts of his personality and nature but he is such an organized whole that no one can see, know and understand the whole of the inner thinking of the most dedicated person nor the outer deeds that he performed when alive and active.

He was the fittest and the most competent person to write the treatise called *Arthashāstra* as he practically proved that unlimited finance can be raised, controlled and redoubled within a limited span of time; with limited resources and while engaged in different battles at different places and while busy in solving other visible and invisible tough tangles.

Reading the books and learning the lessons and teachings by trot is not alright. It is rather the weakest sort of learning. Their assimilation, coordination and timely use in proper manner at opportune time in proper order are really important. It is possible only with a tranquil mind and deep insight which can be immensely developed to know people and solve problems.

4

Chānakya Sutra

Chānakya was an original thinker. He had insight and possessed a tranquil mind. With that great possession, he expressed his teachings in one liner "*Sutras*" or aphorisms. These are the small or prosaic statements but are so rich in denotations and connotations that they appear to be the brightest, largest and most shapely pearls, hence, the costliest. Each one has come out of true and long practical experience of life. Hence, they are as large as life itself; as colourful and varied as life itself because they cover all from royal personalities to paupers; from saints to thieves; from most humble and gentle to deceitful and notorious.

Chānakya has felt, painted and theorized every aspect of life as he saw and felt. The grand success, popularity and immortality of these *sutras* lie in the fact that they are true and present the persons and their characters in true light. They are true even now. The suggestions and teachings have given success to umpteen number of people down the millenniums. They are as living and true as they were at the time of Chānakya.

Chānakya *sutras* present a vivid picture of the society, of people, their aspirations, their character, and their thinking.

Selected Chānakya Sutras

➢ *Sukhasya moolam dharmam*: Religiosity is the basis of happiness, & righteousness is the root of happiness.

- *Dharmasya moolam artham*: Wealth is the basic supporting element for religion & wealth is the root of righteousness.

- *Arthasya moolam rājyam*: Governance is the fundamental requirement for wealth & the state is the root of wealth.

- *Rājasya moolam indriya vijayam*: Control over self is the basic need for governance or creation of kingship & victory over senses is the root of the state.

- *Indriyajayasya moolam vinayah*: Humility is the root of sense control.

- *Vinayasya moolam vriddhopa sevā*: Worship of elders is the root of humility.

- *Vriddha sevāyā vigyānam*: Wisdom results from the worship of elders.

- *Vigyānena ātmānam sampādayet*: With wisdom, one can prosper.

- *Sampādita ātmā jita ātmā bhavati*: The prosperous one becomes the victorious one.

- *Jit-ātmā sarva-arthaih sanjute*: The victorious one attains all the riches.

- *Artham sampad prakriti sampadam karoti*: Economic prosperity creates prosperity for the people.

- *Prakriti sampadā hya nāyakam api rājyam niyate*: If the people are prosperous, even a leaderless state can be governed.

- *Prakriti kopah sarva kopebhyoh gariyān*: Nature's fury is the greatest of all furies.

- *Āpatsu sneh sanyuktam mitram*: One who is affectionate in difficulties is the friend.

- *Mitra sangrahane balam sampadyate*: In the acquisition of allies, one develops strength.

- *Balvān labdha lābhe prayatate*: The strong one tries to get what has not been attained.

➤ *Alabdha lābho na ālasya*: The lazy one does not get what has not been obtained.

➤ *Alasasya labdham api rakshatum na shakyate*: The lazy one cannot guard even what has been begotten.

➤ *Na cha ālasasya rakshitam vivardhate*: Anything looked after by the lazy does not grow.

➤ *Na bhrityān prshayati*: (The lazy one) cannot even command servants.

➤ *Tantram swa-vishaye krityeh vāyattam*: Deployment of the fourfold policy (conciliation, donation, division and punishment) in one's own country is internal administration.

➤ *Āwāpo mandal nivishta*: Foreign policy is deployment of the same (fourfold means) towards other and (neighbouring) states.

➤ *Sandhi-vigrah yoni mandalah*: Neighbouring states are the source of treaties and hostilities.

➤ *Niti Shāstra ānugo rājā*: A ruler should follow political science.

➤ *Anantar prakritih shatruh*: A ruler with contiguous territory is a rival.

➤ *Yekānta aritam mitram ishyate*: The ruler next to the adjoining one is to be deemed a friend.

➤ *Hetutah shatru mitrae bhavishyatah*: Friendship and enmity result from some cause.

➤ *Heeyamānah sandhim kurvita*: The one who is facing defeat should make peace.

➤ *Tejo hi sandhān hetuh tadarthānām*: Power is the cause of an alliance.

➤ *Na tapta loho lohena sandhiyate*: Unheated metal does not coalesce with metal.

➤ *Balwān hinena vigrihneeyāt*: The strong ruler should fight the weak.

➤ *Na jyāyasā samena wā*: One should not fight with a superior or equal.

➤ *Gaj-pāda yuddham eva bal-vad-vigrahah*: Fight with a stronger one is like that of the infantry with the elephant force.

➤ *Agni vadrā jānam āshrayet*: A ruler (the head of a state or organization) should be approached like fire.

➤ *Rāgyah pratikulam na ācharet*: One should not act against the ruler.

➤ *Uddhat veshdharo na bhavet* : One should not wear provocative clothes.

➤ *Na deva charitam charet*: One should not imitate the ways of gods.

➤ *Dvayoh peeshah yatoh dvaidhi bhāvam kurvit*: When two persons quarrel, one should maintain an attitude of duplicity.

➤ *Na vayasan parasya kāryā vāpti*: One addicted to vices does not accomplish tasks.

➤ *Indriya vashavarti chaturang wā api vinshayati*: Even one with a fourfold army is destroyed if he is a slave of the senses.

➤ *Nāsti kāryam dyuta pravritasya*: One addicted to gambling does not accomplish anything.

➤ *Mrigayā parasya dharma arthau vināshyatah*: The ruler addicted to hunting loses his righteousness and wealth.

➤ *Artha anveshnā na vyasaneshu ganyate*: Desire for wealth is not considered a vice.

➤ *Na kāma āsaktasya kārya anushthānam*: The sensuous lustful ruler cannot perform his task.

➤ *Agni dāhād api vishishtam vākya pārusgyam*: Sting of words is stronger than the burning of fire.

➤ *Danda pārushyāt sarva jana dveshyo bhavati*: By giving excessively cruel punishment, (the ruler) becomes hated by all.

- *Artha toshinam shrih parityajyati*: Prosperity abandons one who is satisfied with wealth.
- *Amitro danda niti āmāyattah*: An enemy should be won over and controlled politically.
- *Danda niti adhishtan prājāh sanrakshati*: In accordance with the law of punishment, the ruler protects the people.
- *Dandah sampadā yojayati*: Punishment enhances one's riches.
- *Danda abhāve mantra varga abhāvah*: In the absence of a definite and fixed rule for punishment, ministers scatter.
- *Na danda akāryāni kurvanti*: Because of the fear of punishment, people do not do things which should not be done.
- *Danda nitim āmāyattam ātma rakshanam*: The protection of ministers depends on the practise of punishing culprits.
- *Ātmani rakshite sarvam rakshitam bhavati*: By self-protection, all are protected.
- *Ātma yattau vriddhi vināshau*: Prosperity and decay depend on oneself.
- *Dando hi vigyāne praneeyate*: The punishment should be announced wisely after adequate deliberation.
- *Durbalo api rājā na avamantvyah*: A ruler, even if weak, should not be despised.
- *Nāsti agnih daurbalyam*: Fire has no weakness.
- *Kāryam purush kārena lakshyam sampadyate*: A task attains its objective through human effort.
- *Purush kāram anuvartate daivam*: Fortune follows human effort.
- *Daivam vinā ati prayatnam karoti yat tad viphalam*: Without God's grace, even excessive effort proves fruitless.
- *Asamāhitasya vrittih nu vidyate*: One who is not calm and collected cannot accomplish tasks.

➤ *Purvam nishchitya pashchāt kāryam ārambhayet*: One should decide first and then commence the task.

➤ *Kārya antare deergha sutratā na kartavyā*: There should be no delay in the undertaking of a new task after completing one.

➤ *Na chala chitasya kāryam vāpti*: The fickle-minded one does not accomplish tasks.

➤ *Hasta gatā avamānanāt kārya vyatikramo bhavati*: If what is obtained is despised, things go awry.

➤ *Dosha varjitāni kāryani durlabhāni*: Flawless jobs are rare.

➤ *Duh anubandham kāryam na ārambhayet*: A work which is obstacle-ridden should not be started.

➤ *Kāla vit kāryam sādhayet*: One who knows the opportune time accomplishes the task.

➤ *Kālāti-kramāt kāla yeva phalam pivati*: Due to lapse of time, time itself consumes the fruit.

➤ *Kshanam prati kāla vichhedam na kuryāt sarva krityeshu*: In all tasks, one should not delay even for a moment.

➤ *Desha phala vibhāgau kāryam ārambhayet*: One should commence a work after understanding the country and the consequences.

➤ *Daivaheenam kāryam susādham api duhsādham bhavati*: Without God's grace, even an easy task becomes difficult to accomplish.

➤ *Nitigyo desha kālau pariksheta*: The wise one should consider the interests of the country, the people and the time.

➤ *Parikshya kārini shrih chiramtishthati*: Prosperity lasts long for one who acts after proper consideration.

➤ *Sarvāshcha sampadah sarva upāyena parigrahet*: All types of riches should be amassed by all means.

➤ *Bhāgya vantam parikshya kārinam shrih parityajati*: Prosperity forsakes even a lucky one, if he acts without foresight.

- *Gyān anumānaih cha parikshā kartavyāh*: Examination and analysis of everything should be done with reference to what is known and what is to be inferred.

- *Yo asmin karmani kushalastam tasminna yeva yojayet*: Everyone should be yoked to the task for which he is befitted.

- *Duhsādham api susādham karotya upāya yagyah* : The one who knows the means makes the impossible possible.

- *Agyāninā kritam api na bahu mantvyam*: What is done by an unintelligent person should not be rated high.

- *Yadrichhikatvāt krimih api rupāntarāni karoti* : Sometimes, due to fortuitous circumstances even a worm assumes different forms, and is metamorphosed.

- *Siddhah yeva kāryasya prakāshanam kartavyam*: Only accomplished deeds should be publicized.

- *Gyānāvatām api daiva mānush doshāt kāryāni dushyanti*: Even the affairs of the learned go awry due to defective destiny and human interference.

- *Daivam shānti karmanāpratisddhavyam*: Destiny has to be counteracted through propitiatory deeds.

- *Mānushih kārya vipattimkaushalena vinivāryet*: Man-made obstacles should be overcome through one's skill.

- *Kārya vipatau doshān varnayanti bālishāh*: When things get too difficult, the childish describe the handicaps.

- *Kārya ārthinā dākshinyam na kartavyam*: Those who seek to achieve things should show no mercy.

- *Ksheerārthi vatso māturuddhah pratihanti*: The milk-seeking calf strikes at the mother's udders.

- *Aprayatnāt kārya vipattih bhavet*: Due to lack of effort tasks fail.

- *Na daiva pramānām kārya siddhih*: Those who blindly believe in destiny do not achieve anything.

- *Kārya vāhyo na poshatya āshritān*: An inactive person cannot protect those who seek refuge in him.

➤ *Yah kāryam na pashyanti sah andhah*: He who does not see action is blind.

➤ *Pratyaksha paroksha anumānaih kāryāni parikshayet*: Things should be examined with reference to facts patent and latent, and inferences.

➤ *Aparikshya kārinam shrih parityajyati*: Prosperity forsakes one who does things without proper examination.

➤ *Parkshya tāryāh vipattih*: Danger should be overcome after proper analysis.

➤ *Swashaktim gyātvā kāryam ārambhayet*: One should begin a venture after assessing one's strength.

➤ *Swajanam tarpayitvā yah sheshabhoji sah amritbhoji*: He feeds on nectar, who first feeds his people and then takes his food.

➤ *Sarva anushthān ādāya mukhāni vardhanti*: By undertaking all kinds of activities, the ways to profit develop.

➤ *Nāsti bhiroh kārya chintā*: The cowards do not worry about action.

➤ *Swāminah sheelam gyātvā kāryārthi kāryam sādhayet*: The favour-seeker accomplishes his end after knowing the nature of his master.

➤ *Dhenoh sheelagyah ksheeram bhungakte*: The one who knows the cows' nature gets the milk.

➤ *Kshudre guhya prakāshanam ātmavān na kuryāt*: A good one should not reveal a secret to a mean one.

➤ *Āshritaih apya avamanyate mridu swabhāvah*: The soft-natured one is disregarded even by those dependent on him.

➤ *Teekshna dandah sarve ruddhe janiya bhavati*: The one who metes out severe punishment creates agitation in everyone.

➤ *Yathāh dandakāri syāt*: Apt punishment should be meted out.

➤ *Alpa sāram shrutvantam api na bahu manyate lokah*: A weak ruler, even if learned, is not respected by people.

➤ *Atibhārah purusham avasādayati*: Excessive burden overpowers a person.

➤ *Yah sansadi pardosham shansati sah swa dosham prakhyāpayati*: He who speaks of other's faults in an assembly proclaims his own defect.

➤ *Yat amānam yeva nāshayatya na ātmavatām kopah*: One who cannot control himself is destroyed by his anger.

➤ *Nāsya prāpyam satyavatām*: Nothing is unattainable by the truthful.

➤ *Sāhasena kārya siddhih bhavati*: With adventurous attempts tasks are accomplished.

➤ *Vyasan ārto vismaratya smaren*: The one troubled by calamities forgets them the moment they disappear.

➤ *Nāstya anantarāyah kāla vikshepe*: When opportunities are lost, obstacles definitely arise.

➤ *Asansaya vināshāt sansay vināshah shreyān*: Doubtful ruin is better than definite ruin.

➤ *Par dhanāni niksheptuh kevalam swārtha*: Custody of others' riches is undertaken purely out of selfishness.

➤ *Dānam dharmah*: Donation is righteousness.

➤ *Nāyah āgato atharvad viparito anarth bhāvah*: The opposite (i.e. non-donation) forebodes disaster, like wealth of the ignoble.

➤ *Yo dharma arthau na vivardhayati sa kāmah*: That wealth is lust which does not increase virtue.

➤ *Tad viparito anartha sevi*: The wealth that is acting against virtue, is courting disaster.

➤ *Riju swabhāva aparo janeshu durlabhah*: Honest and upright people are rare.

- *Avamānena āgatam aishwaryam avamanyate sādhuh*: The virtuous one despises prosperity attained through ignominy.

- *Bahunā api gunāni yeko doshah grasati*: A single defect overshadows many qualities.

- *Mahātmanā parena sāhasam na kartvyam*: Rash aggression should not be committed against a great and noble enemy.

- *Kadāchid api charitram na langhayet*: The bounds of good conduct should never be crossed.

- *Kshudhārtho na trinam charati singhah*: Though hungry, yet a lion does not graze grass.

- *Prānād api pratyayo rakshitah*: Trust and promises should be kept even by sacrificing one's life.

- *Pishunah shrotā putra darai api tyajyate*: A slanderous listener is forsaken even by his wife and children.

- *Bālād apya artham jātam shrinuyāt*: Meaningful words, even from a child, should be listened to.

- *Satyam apya ashradheyam na vadet*: Don't speak that truth which will not be believed.

- *Na alpa doshād bahugunāh tyajyante*: Many qualities are not to be overlooked for a minor defect.

- *Vipashchit swa api sulabhā doshāh*: Faults are common even among the learned like Vipashchit.

- *Nāsti ratnam akhanditam*: There is no unbroken diamond.

- *Maryādā atitam na kadāchid api vishwaset*: Excessive courtesy should never be trusted.

- *Apriye kritam priyam api dveshyam bhavati*: In the case of an enemy, even a good gesture becomes harmful.

- *Namantya api tulā kotih kupa odak kshayam karoti*: Even while bending, the mouth of the pitcher depletes the water in the well.

- *Satām matam nāti kramet*: One should not act against the advice of the good.

- *Gunavad āshraya abhinnah guna api guni bhavati*: Through the association of the good, even one without virtue becomes virtuous.

- *Ksheer āshritam jalam ksheeram yeva bhavati*: Water mixed with milk becomes milk.

- *Mrit pinda api pātali gandham utpādayati*: Even a lump of earth can produce the smell of the trumpet flower.

- *Rajatam kanak sangāt kanakam bhavati*: Silver in contact with gold becomes golden.

- *Upkartah apkartum ikshatya budhah*: The foolish wish to do harm to those who do good.

- *Na pāpa karmanām ākrosh bhayam*: Evil doers are not afraid of criticism.

- *Utsāh vatām shatru api vashi bhavanti*: The enthusiastic ones even win over enemies.

- *Vikram dhanāh rājānah*: Valour is the wealth of rulers.

- *Nāsti ālasasya ahikām ushmikam*: A lazy one cannot get happiness in this world or the other.

- *Nirutsāhād daivam patati*: Due to lack of effort, fortune fails.

- *Matasya arthiva jalam upya ujyārtham hrihiniyārth*: Utilizable resources should be captured, as the fisherman catches fish from water.

- *Avishwastateshu vishwāso na kartavyah*: The untrustworthy should not be trusted.

- *Visham visham yeva sarva kālam*: Poison is always poison.

- *Artha samādāne vairinām sanga yeva na kartavyah*: In the acquisition of wealth, the association of enemies should be avoided.

➤ *Artha sidhau vairinam na vishwaset*: Even after wealth has been acquired, an enemy should not be trusted.

➤ *Artha ādhin yeva niyat sambandhah*: Relationship depends on wealth.

➤ *Shatruh api sutah sakhā rakshitah*: A friend, even if he be the enemy's son, should be protected.

➤ *Neechasya matih na dātavyā*: The low-minded should not be given good advice.

➤ *Teshu vishwāso na kartvyah*: They, the low-minded, should never be trusted.

➤ *Supujito api durjanah peedaytya yeva*: The evil one harms, even if treated well.

➤ *Chandan ādin api dāvo agnih dahatyeva*: The forest fire burns even trees like sandalwood.

➤ *Kadā api purusham nāvamanyeta*: No one should ever be disrespected.

➤ *Kshantavyam iti purusham na bādhet*: One who is to be pardoned should not be harassed.

➤ *Bhatrā adhikam rahasya yuktam vaktum ichchhintya buddhayah*: The foolish wish to speak out what was spoken in secret by the master.

➤ *Anurāga astu phalena suchyate*: Love is indicated by its fruit.

➤ *Āgyā phalam aishwaryam*: A command or order of the ruler should result in prosperity.

➤ *Dātvyam api bālishah parikleshena dāsyati*: The foolish give what is to be given with great difficulty.

➤ *Mahad aishwaryam prāpyāpya dhritimān vinashyati*: Even after attaining great prosperity, the one without fortitude perishes.

➤ *Nāstya dhrite raihikā mushmikam*: The one without fortitude does not enjoy anything be it materially or spiritually.

➤ *Nah durjanaih sah sansargah kartavyah*: Don't associate with bad people.

➤ *Shaunda hasta gatam payo-apyava-manyet*: Even milk in the hands of a drunkard acquires disrepute.

➤ *Kārya sankateva artha vyavasāyini buddhih*: Intellect is that which can decide on action in difficulties.

➤ *Mita bhojanam swāsthyam*: Moderate eating is healthy.

➤ *Pathyam apathyam wā ajirne nāshniyāt*: In indigestion, no food, wholesome or otherwise, should be taken.

➤ *Jirna bhojinam vyādhih na upasarpati*: Disease does not touch one who digests his food.

➤ *Jeerna sharire vardhamānam vyādhim na upekshet*: In an old body, a growing disease should not be neglected.

➤ *Ajirna bhojanam dukham*: It is painful to eat in indigestion.

➤ *Dānam nidhānam anugāmi*: Donation follows wealth.

➤ *Patutare trishnā pare sulabha mati sandhānam*: It is easy to deceive the clever and the greedy.

➤ *Trishnāh matih chhādyate*: Greed clouds the intellect.

➤ *Kārya bahutve bahuphal māyātikam kuryāt*: When there are many difficult tasks, abundant rewards should be made the incentive.

➤ *Swayameva āvaskanna kāryam nirikshet*: Secret tasks should be scrutinized by the person himself.

➤ *Dharmena dhāryate lokah*: The world is borne by righteousness.

➤ *Pretam api dharma adharma avanugachhatah*: Vice and virtue pursue even the departed spirit.

➤ *Dayā dharmasya janmabhumih*: Kindness is the mother of righteousness.

➤ *Dharma mole satya dāne*: Truth and charity are the roots of righteousness.

- *Dharmena jayati lokān*: One can conquer the worlds with righteousness.
- *Mrityuh api dharma nishthah rakshati*: Even death protects the righteous.
- *Dharma ādi viparitam pāpam yatra prasajyate tatra dharma awamatim mahati prasajyate*: Where a sinful act contrary to righteousness is propagated, great disregard for righteousness and religion is propagated.
- *Upasthita vināshānām prakrityā kārena kāryena lakshyate*: The state of those about to perish is seen through their appearance and deeds.
- *Ātma vināsham suchayatya adharma buddhih*: The evil intellect suggests self-destruction.
- *Swajaneshwa atikraman na kartavyah*: One should not disrespect one's people.
- *Mātā api dushtā tyājyā*: Even a mother, if cruel, has to be given up.
- *Swa hasto api visha digdhah chhedah*: One's own hand, if poisoned, has to be cut off.
- *Paro api cha hito bandhuh*: A benefactor, even if he be a foreigner, is a kinsman.
- *Kakshādapya aushadham grihyate*: Medicine can be extracted even from dry grass.
- *Nāst chaureshu vishwāsah*: Thieves should not be trusted.
- *Apratikāreshva anādaro na kartvyah*: Easy tasks should not be neglected.
- *Vyasanam manāg api bādhate*: Even a small weakness creates trouble.
- *Amar vadarth jātam arjayet*: One should earn wealth as if one is immortal.
- *Arthavān sarva lokasya bahumatah*: The wealthy are respected by all.

➤ *Mahendrah api arthaheenam na bahu manyate lokah*: The world does not respect one without riches, even if he be Indra (the king of gods).

➤ *Dāridtam khalu purushasya jeevitam maranam*: Poverty of a person is death while living.

➤ *Virupo arthvān surupo*: Even an ugly one, if rich, is considered handsome.

➤ *Adātāram apya arthavantam arthino na tyajanti*: The aid-seekers do not give up the rich one, even if he is not a donor.

➤ *Akulino api dhani kulina ādi vishitah*: Even a low born, if rich, will be deemed superior to the high born.

➤ *Nāstya avamān bhayam anāryasya*: The ignoble have no fear of shame.

➤ *Na chetan vatām vritti bhayam*: The intelligent have no fear about their livelihood.

➤ *Na jitendriyānām vishaya bhayam*: Those who have controlled their senses are not afraid of sensual objects.

➤ *Na kritārthānām maran bhayam*: The contented have no fear of death.

➤ *Kasya chid artham swamiva manyate sādhuh*: The good one considers others' wealth as his own.

➤ *Par vibhaveshwar ādaro na kartavyah*: One should not be desirous of others' prosperity.

➤ *Par vibheshwa ādaro api nāsha moolam*: Desire for others' prosperity is the root of destruction.

➤ *Palālam api par-dravyam na hartavyam*: Another's wealth, even if it be husk, should not be stolen.

➤ *Par dravya apaharanam ātma dravya nāsha hetuh*: Stealing others' wealth leads to loss of one's own.

➤ *Na chauryātma param mrityu pāshah*: There is no greater bond to sorrow than stealing.

> *Yavāguh api prāna dhāram karoti kāle*: Even gruel, obtained in time, helps maintain life.

> *Na mrit aushadham prayojanam*: To the dead, medicine is of no use.

> *Sam kāle swayam api prabhutvasya prayojanam bhavati*: At the appropriate time, prosperity is useful.

> *Neechasya vidyā pāpa karmani yojayanti*: Learning of the low-minded is yoked to sinful deeds.

> *Payah pānam visha vardhanam bhujangasya na amrit syāt*: Feeding a snake with milk increases its venom, no nectar is produced.

> *Na hi dhānya samo hya artham*: No other wealth can equal grain.

> *Na kshudhā samah shatruh*: There is no enemy equal to hunger.

> *Akrite niyat kshut*: One who does wrong things has to inevitably suffer hunger.

> *Nāsya tasya abhakshyam kshudhi tasya*: There is nothing uneatable for a hungry one.

> *Indriyāni jarā vasham kurvanti*: Over-indulgence in senses ages one fast.

> *Sa anukrosham bhartāram jivet*: One should earn one's livelihood, serving a compassionate master.

> *Lubdha sevi pāvakeh chhayā khadyotam dhamati* : One who serves a miserly master is like one who fans the firefly to get fire.

> *Visheshagya swāminam āshrayet*: One should serve a learned master.

> *Nāstya ahankār samah shatruh*: There is no enemy equal to an arrogant man.

> *Sansadi shatrum na parikroshet*: In an assembly, an enemy should not be criticized.

- *Shatruvyasanam shravan sukham*: An enemy's trouble is pleasant to hear.
- *Adhanasya buddhih na vidyate*: A poor one has no intellect.
- *Hitam apya dhanasya vākyam na grihyate*: A poor man's word, even if apt, is not heard.
- *Adhanah swa bhāryāyā apya avamanyate*: The poor one is despised by his own wife.
- *Pushpaheenam sahakāram api na upāsate bhramarāh*: Bees do not go to the flowerless mango tree.
- *Vidyā dhanam adhanānām*: Learning is wealth to the poor.
- *Vidyā chauraih api na grāhyānām*: The wealth of learning cannot be stolen by thieves.
- *Vidayā khyāpitā jayātih*: Fame is glorified by learning.
- *Yashah shariram na vinashayti*: The body or the person who performs meritorious deeds never dies.
- *Yah parārtham upasarpati sa satpururshah*: He is the good one who moves forward to help others.
- *Indriyānām prathamam shāshtram*: Sense organs are the first books that one learns from and through.
- *Ashāstra kārya vrittau shāstra ankusham nivārayati*: The good of learning corrects those engaged in unworthy deeds.
- *Neechasya vidyā na upetavyā*: One should not use the learning of the low-minded.
- *Malechchha bhāshanam na shikshet*: Language of the bad should not be used.
- *Malechchhānām api suvrittam grāhyam*: Good customs of even low people should be adopted.
- *Gune na matsarah kartavyah*: One should not envy others' good qualities.
- *Shatruh api suguno grāhya*: A good quality should be learnt even from an enemy.

- *Vishādapya amritam grāhyam*: Nectar should be extracted even from poison.
- *Avawasthāyā purushah sammānyate*: A person is honoured according to his age and status.
- *Na stri ratna samam ratnam*: There is no jewel equal to a good woman.
- *Ayashobhayam bhayeshu*: Fear of a bad name is the greatest fear.
- *Nāst ālasasya shāstra āgamah*: An idle one cannot learn the sciences.
- *Adravya prayatno bālukā kwathanāna anyah*: Attempting a task without resources is to plough the sand.
- *Na mahājanah hāsah kartavyah*: One should not laugh at great people.
- *Kārya anurupah prayatnah*: Effort should befit the task.
- *Pātra anurupam dānam*: Donation should befit recipient.
- *Vaya anurupo veshah*: Dress should befit age.
- *Swāmi anukulo bhrityah*: A servant should obey the master.
- *Guru vasha anuvarti shishyah*: A student should obey the teacher.
- *Pitri vasha anuvaryi putrah*: A son should obey the father.
- *Ati upachārah shankitvyah*: Excessive courtesy should be suspected.
- *Swāmina yeva anuvartate*: The master should always be obeyed.
- *Mātri tādito vatso mātaram yeva anurodati*: A child beaten by the mother cries only before the mother.
- *Sneha vatah swalpo hi roshah*: The anger of the affectionate is short-lived.
- *Ātma chhidram na pashyati par chhidram yeva pashyati bālishah*: The fool sees others' faults, not his own.

➤ *Sa-upachārah kaitavah*: Cunning accompanies courtesy.

➤ *Kāmyaih vishshaih upacharanam upachārah*: Provision of desirable services is courtesy.

➤ *Chir parichitānām upachārah shankitavyah*: Excessive courtesy from long-known people is suspicious.

➤ *Gauh dushkarāshva sahastra ādekākini shreyasi*: Even an ordinary cow is superior to a thousand dogs.

➤ *Swo mayurādadya kapoto varah*: A pigeon today is better than a peacock tomorrow.

➤ *Ati sango dosham utpādayati*: Excessive companionship creates trouble.

➤ *Sarvan jayet akrodhah*: The one without anger wins over all.

➤ *Na asti pishācham aishwaryam*: There is some devilish element in prosperity.

➤ *Nāsti dhanvatām shubh karmeshu shramah*: It is not difficult for the rich to do good deeds.

➤ *Nāsti gati shramo yānvatām*: The ones who travel by airways do not feel the weariness of journeys.

➤ *Gurunām mātā gariyashi*: A mother is the greatest teacher.

➤ *Sarva avasthāsu mātā bhartvyā*: In all circumstances, the mother should be looked after.

➤ *Vaidushyam alankārena achchhādyate*: Wisdom is clothed in figures of speech.

➤ *Strinām bhushanam lajjā*: Modesty is the ornament of women.

➤ *Viprānām bhushanam vedah*: Knowledge is the ornament of the learned.

➤ *Sarveshā bhushanam dharmam*: Righteousness is the ornament of all.

➤ *Bhushanānām bhushanam savinayā vidyā*: Learning, accompanied by humility, is the ornament of ornaments.

- *Un-updravam desham avaset*: One should live in a country free from strife.
- *Sādhu janah bahulo deshah*: The right country is that where a lot of good people live.
- *Rāgyo vetavyam sarva kālam*: The ruler should be feared all the time.
- *Na rāgyah param daivatam*: There is no god greater than the ruler.
- *Suduram api dahati rāja vanhvi*: The ruler's wrath reduces one to ashes even at a long distance.
- *Rikta hasto na rājānam abhigachhet*: One should not approach a ruler empty-handed.
- *Gurum cha daivam cha*: One should not go to a teacher or a deity empty handed.
- *Kutumbino bhetyam*: Members of the royal family should be feared.
- *Gantavyam cha sadā rājkulam*: One should often visit the royal court.
- *Rāja purushaih sambandham kuryāt*: One should have friendly connections with the ruling elite.
- *Rāja dāsi na sevitavyā*: The king's maid should not be courted.
- *Jana padārtham grāmam tyajet*: For the country's sake, the interests of the village should be forsaken.
- *Grāmartham kutumbasya tyajet*: For the sake of the village, the interests of the family should be forsaken.
- *Swa dāsi parigraho hi dāsa bhāvah*: Possession of the maid servant enslaves one.
- *Upasthita vināshah pathya vākyam na shrinoti*: The one for whom destruction is imminent does not listen to wholesome advice.

- *Mātaram eva vatsāh sukha dukhāni kartāram yeva anugachchhati*: As children follow their mother, pleasure and pain follow the doer of actions.

- *Tila mātra apya upakāram shailavan manyate sādhuh*: The good one considers even a tiny help rendered to him as very big.

- *Swalpam upakār krite prati upakāram kartum āryo na swipiti*: The noble one does not forget to render great help in return for the smallest aid received.

- *Na kadāpi devat avamantvyā*: Gods should never be despised.

- *Na chakshusah samam jyotih asti*: There is no light equal to eyesight.

- *Chakshuh hi sharirānām netā*: The eye is the leader of the embodied being.

- *Na apsu mutram kuryāt*: One should not urinate in water.

- *Na nagno jalam pravishet*: One should not enter water in the nude.

- *Yathā shariram tathā gyānam*: The mind will be as healthy as the body.

- *Agneya agnim na nikshipet*: One should not deposit fire in fire. (One should not express anger at the mighty.)

- *Tapaswinah pujyaneeyā*: Saints should be worshipped.

- *Par dārā na gachchheta*: Others' wives should not be sought.

- *Na veda bāhyo dharmah*: There is no righteous duty not specified in the learned scriptures.

- *Swargam nayati sunritam*: Truth and sweet words lead one to heaven.

- *Na asti satyāt param tapah*: There is no penance greater than the observance of truth.

➤ *Satyam swargasya sādhanam*: Truth is the means to heaven.

➤ *Satyena dhāryate lokah*: The world is borne by truth.

➤ *Satyāt devo varshati*: Because of truth, God gives rain.

➤ *Na anritāt pātakam param*: There is no greater sin than falsehood.

➤ *Na mimāmsayā guruvah*: Teachers should not be criticized.

➤ *Khalatvam na upeyāt*: Villainy should not be tolerated.

➤ *Na asti khalasya mitram*: The wicked have no friends.

➤ *Loka yātrā daridram bādhate*: The poor find it hard to live.

➤ *Ati shuro dān shurah*: The most valiant is the valiant giver.

➤ *Guru deva brāhmaneshu bhaktih bhushanam*: Devotion to teacher, God and the learned is adornment for all.

➤ *Sarvasya bhushanam vinayah*: Humility is everyone's adornment.

➤ *Akulino api vinitah kulinād vishishtah*: Even a low-born one, if humble, is superior to an arrogant high-born one.

➤ *Āchār āyuh vardhate kirtih cha*: Good living enhances life-span and reputation.

➤ *Priyam apya ahitam na vadah*: Sweet words, if inapt, should not be spoken.

➤ *Bahujan virddham yekam na anuvartet*: One who is opposed by many people should not be followed.

➤ *Na durjaneshu bhāga adheyah kartvyah*: One's fortune should not be linked to evil ones.

➤ *Na kritātheshu neecheshu sambandhah*: One should not associate with the low-minded, even if they are successful.

➤ *Rina shatru vyādhi avasheshah na kartavyah*: Nothing should be allowed to remain in the case of debts, enemies, and disease.

- *Bhutya anuvartanam purushasya rasāyanam*: Treading the right path is man's best medicine.
- *Na arthishwa avagyā kāryā*: Aid-seekers should not be hated.
- *Dushkaram karma kāryitvā kartārah avamanyate neechah*: The evil one alter propelling evil action, derides the doer.
- *Na akritagyasya narakānni vartanam*: The ungrateful cannot escape hell.
- *Jihvā yattau buddhi vināshau*: Development and decline depend on the tongue.
- *Visha amritayoh ākari jihvā*: The tongue is the storehouse of poison and nectar.
- *Priya vādino na shatruh*: The sweet spoken have no enemies.
- *Stutā api devatāh tushtayanti*: Even gods, when praised, are pleased.
- *Anritam api durvachanam chiram tishthati*: Evil speech, though unintended, remains long in memory.
- *Rāja dvishtam na cha vaktavyam*: Nothing seen in the palace about the ruler should be spoken ever.
- *Shruti sukhāt kokilā alāpāt tushyanti*: Words should be spoken which delight the ear like koel's cooing.
- *Swadharma kartuh sat purushah*: A man who does his duty is a good and righteous man.
- *Na asti arthino gaurava*: Beggars cannot have dignity.
- *Strinām bhushanam saubhāgyam*: Husband is a woman's ornament.
- *Shatruh api pātaneeyā vrittih*: Even an enemy should not be deprived of his livelihood.
- *Aprayatna odakam kshetram*: The land where water is easily available is the right field to be cultivated.

➤ *Arandam avalambya kunjaram na kopayet*: One should not anger the elephant with the support of the castor plant, which means that one should not anger the mighty with the support of the weak.

➤ *Ati pravriddhā shālmali vāran stambho na bhavati*: Even if well-grown, the silk-cotton tree does not become a fit pillar to bind an elephant.

➤ *Ati deergho api karnikāro na musali*: However big, the *karnikāra* tree cannot be used to make clubs.

➤ *Ati deepto api khadyoto na pāwakah*: Even the brightest firefly is not fire.

➤ *Na prabhutvam guna hetuh*: Mere growth cannot create quality.

➤ *Gatānugatiko lokah*: People are tradition-bound.

➤ *Yam anujivet tam na apvadet*: One should not speak ill of the person who is responsible for one's livelihood.

➤ *Tapah sārah indriya nigrahah*: The essence of penance is control of senses.

➤ *Durlabha stri bandhanān mokshah*: Liberation out of woman's shackle is difficult.

➤ *Na cha strinām purush parikshā*: Women cannot judge men.

➤ *Na putra sansparshāt param sukham*: No pleasure is greater than the touch of one's children.

➤ *Vivāde dharmam anusmaret*: In debate, what is right should be remembered.

➤ *Nishā ante kāryam chintayet*: Every morning, the day's tasks should be planned.

➤ *Upashthita vināsho durnayam manyate*: He, whose destruction is imminent, plans evil action.

➤ *Ksheera arthinah kim karinyā*: What is the use of an elephant for one in need of milk?

- *Na dān samam vashyam*: There is no attraction equal to a gift.
- *Parāya teshu utakanthām na kuryāt*: One should not desire others' property.
- *Asat samriddih asad bhih yeva bhujyate*: Evil riches are enjoyed by only the evil-minded.
- *Nimba phalam kākaih yeva bhujyate*: The bitter *neem* fruit is eaten only by crows.
- *Na ambodhih trishnām peehati*: The oceans cannot quench thirst.
- *Bālukā api swagunam āshrayet*: Even sand conforms to its quality.
- *Santo astasu na ramante*: Good people do not enjoy the company of evil ones.
- *Hansah pretavane na ramate*: Swans do not like to stay in cremation grounds.
- *Arthārtham pravartate lokah*: The world functions for the sake of money.
- *Āshayā badhyate lokah*: All worldly beings are bound by desire.
- *Na cha āshā pariah shrih sah tishthati*: Prosperity does not slay with one ever immersed in desire.
- *Āshāpare na dhairyam*: Those who have excessive desire have no firmness.
- *Rāja āgyā nāti langhayet*: The ruler's order should not be disobeyed.
- *Yathā āgyāptam tathā kuryāt*: Whatever has been ordered by the ruler should be carried out.
- *Dharmādapi vyavahāro gareeyān*: Proper behaviour is more important than being virtuous.
- *Ātmā hi vyahārasya sākshi*: The soul is the witness of a transaction.

> *Kuta sākshino narake patanti*: False witnesses fall into hell.

> *Prachchhanna pāpānām sākshini mahābhutāni*: Witnesses of hidden sins are the gross elements.

> *Ātmanah pāpam ātman yeva prakāshayati*: One's sin is revealed by oneself.

> *Vyavahāre antargatam āchārah suchayati*: In behaviour, the outer form indicates the inner core.

> *Ākār samvaranam devānām ashakyam*: To hide one's form is impossible even for the gods.

> *Chore rāja purushebhyo vittam rakshet*: Wealth should be protected from robbers and ruling officials.

Asado mā sad gamaya!
Tamaso mā jyotir gamaya!
Mrityore mā amritam gamaya!
Aum Shāntih! Shāntih! Shāntih!

O God! Lead us from unreal to real,
from untruth to truth.
O God! Lead us from darkness to light.
O God! Lead us from death to immortality.
O God! Let there be peace, peace and peace.

Kautilya Arthshastra

VYAVASHTHÄ CHINTAN
THOUGHTS FOR GOVERNANCE

SECTION II

5

Meaning of Artha, Economy

Chānakya was a shrewd observer of nature, human beings and non-human beings. He had an uncanny ability to co-relate many things wisely to come to a solid and true conclusion. It opened his inner eyes, gave him powerful insight and made him a thoughtful theoretician. This showed others the ways to be followed and means to be adopted not only during his lifetime but till today through his aphorisms and dictums. A seemingly insignificant sight will be sufficient to explain this.

Once the Mauryan forces had to hide in a cave. They were defeated and chased by the big and powerful Magadh Army. There was no food, and the soldiers were starving. They could not come out of the cave either, as there was a threat to their lives. The Magadh Army was still very close to them.

Chānakya saw an ant taking a grain of rice, even though there was no sign of food or grains anywhere. Moreover, the rice grain was cooked. He took that grain. It was freshly cooked and still soft. He ordered the soldiers to search and they found that their enemies had been dining behind the cave. Indeed, they were eating at the ground and were not prepared for a war. They must have been coming there in large groups to take their meal with their weapons collected at different places. As soon as they saw the Mauryans, they escaped leaving behind the weapons, horses, chariots and food to last for weeks. Hungry young Mauryans chased them without engaging in actual battle. They got food and weapons that they needed the most and thus were saved.

Appraisal

To be conscious towards every movement and events taking place all around gives unfathomable inner strength. It takes time, practise and concentration to achieve that rare quality. A person with that ability keeps an eye on everything; overlooks nothing and is never deceived.

Effect

Nothing that happens is meaningless because each incident has a cause behind and at the beginning.

Rights, Duties and Responsibilities of the Governing Body

The *Kautilya Arthashāstra* is not about a subject called Economics that is taught and learnt in schools and colleges. It includes all sorts of disciplined and moral, legal and ethical earnings. It fixes the ways and rules of earning. It does not provide the study of economy in theory; or of the study of the economy of a particular country or section in particular. It is neither theoretical nor practical economics. Moreover, it fixes the ways and means of earning and fulfilling responsibilities towards the governing body including the rights, duties and responsibilities of the governing body or the king.

At the end of the book in the concluding *Prakaran* or chapter, Kautilya declares the meaning of *artha:*

Manushyānām vrittih arthah: the livelihood of human beings is called *artha.*

Manushyavati bhumih iti arthah: the land occupied by human beings is called *artha.*

Tasyāh prithivyā lābha pālana upāyah shāstram artha shāstram iti: The science that discusses and shows ways and means for the procurement and safe use or safety of such lands is called *Arthashāstra.*

In India, this science has been given a very wide scope. It gives ideal teaching that: *Dharma artha virodhena kāmam seveta na nihsukhah syāt*: One should follow the dictates of *dharma* and *artha.* One who moves in the opposite direction is never happy.

➢ To pray for someone in meek words: *tvāmi mam artham arthayate;*

➢ To try to get something: *priyā pravritti nimittam abhyartaye;*

➢ Meaning, cause, purpose, wish, desire: *gyān arthogyān sambandhah shrotum shrotah.*

There are three types of meanings

(a) vāchya, abhivyakt or *abhidhā* (simple, general)

(b) lakshya, lakshanā (symbolic, intentional);

(c) vyangya (ironical, satirical)

➢ Cause, reason, means, that which can be perceived by senses (*roop, rasa, gandh, sparsh, shabda*) *indriyabhyah parāhya arthā arthe bhyashcha param manah*

➢ Proceedings, business, proposal, work (*artho ayam arthāntar bhāvya yeva*)

> Wealth, money, worldly accumulations, one of the pursuits (*apya arth kāmau tasya āstām dharma yeva manishinah*)
> Use, welfare, profit, wholesome deeds (*tathā hi sarve tasya āsan parārthe kaphalā gunāh*)
> Way, type, technique
> To stop; to keep away; annihilate

Arth *āgam*, accumulation of wealth or receiving money is pleasant; *arth upārjanam*, earning money is essential for sustenance; though the people have lost *arth gauravam*. It is the reality, *Arth tattvam*. *Arth dushanam*, extravagant expenditure, must be stopped for balanced living for a long time. Some such people try to evade and search for some substitute or *arth vikalp*.

Chānakya in the *Kautilya Arthshāstram* has given 32 types of *arth*, meanings. It is very interesting to see them. In the wake of popularizing English words we are going far away from such meaningful words. It must be read carefully, all the three: *shabda, sutra* and *arth*. Chānkya says that the livelihood of human beings is called artha; the land inhabited by men is also called artha; and the branch of study that deals with acquiring land, controling it, and keeping it in control is called *Arthshāstra*. That the *Arthshāstra* follows 32 ways to acquire control and manage it. The following are Kautilya's or Chānakya's way of accumulating and managing wealth. In it he is the first management guru that has dealt with the topic in detail and has given the general and uncanny ways for the benefit of all human beings. They are the following:

1. **Adhikaran**: *yama artham adhikritya uchyate tad adhikaranam*; whatever is said authoritatively is called *adhikaran*.

2. **Vidhānam**: *shāstra prakaran anupurvi vidhānam*; to speak according to the situation is called *Vidhān*.

3. **Yogah**: *vākya yojanā yogah*; the construction of a sentence is called yoga; *chatur varnāshramo lokah*.

4. **Padārth**: *padāva adhikah padārthah*; only the meaning of a word is called *padārth*.

5. **Hetvarthah**: *hetuk arth sādhako hetvarthah*, that which proves the meaning, for example: *arth mulau hi dharma kāmau*; religion and sex depend on wealth.

6. **Uddeshah**: *samās vākyam uddeshah*; the statement in a short sentence is called *Uddesh* or purpose, for example, *vidyā vinay hetruh indriya jayah*, learning and humility depends on the control of senses.

7. **Nirdeshah**: *vyās vākyam nirdeshah*, the statement describing a thing in detail is called direction, *nirdesh*.

8. **Upadeshah**: The statement that tells how to behave is called *Upadesh*. For example: one should work according to the scriptures and available finance.

9. **Apadeshah**: *Yevam sāvāhetu apadeshah*, when the statement of another person is quoted, it is called *Apadesh*.

10. **Atideshah**: *Iuktena sādhanam Atideshah*, to prove what is not said with what has been said is called *Atidesh*.

11. **Pradeshah**: *Ivyaktavyena sādhanam Pradeshah*, to prove what is said with what is to be said is called *Pradesh*.

12. **Upamānam**: *Drishtena ādrishtasya sādhanam Upamānam*, to prove the unseen with the seen things is called *Upamāna*.

13. **Arthāpati**: *Yada anukatam arthād āpyate sa Arthapatih*, that which is gained from the unsaid things is called *Arthāpati*.

14. **Sanshayah**: *Ubhayato hetum anarthah sanshayah*, when a thing appears the same to the opposite parties, it is called *Sanshaya*.

15. **Prasangah**: *Prakarnantarena samān arthah Prasangah*; the similarity of meaning with another event is called *Prasang*.

16. **Viparyaya:** *Pratilomena sādhanam viparyayah,* to indicate a thing with opposite statements is called *Viparyaya.*

17. **Vākya Sheshah:** *Yena vākyam samāpyate, sa vākya sheshah,* the closing of a sentence is called *Vākya Shesh.*

18. **Anumatam:** *Par vākyam prati siddham Anumatam,* the statement by another person which has not been opposed is called *Anumatam.*

19. **Vyākhyānam:** *Atishaya varnanā Vyākhyānam,* to prove in different ways, what has already been proved is called *Vyākhyāna.*

20. **Nirvachanam:** *Gunatah shabda nishpatih nirvachanam,* to prove something by giving meaning is called *Nirvachanam.*

21. **Nidarshanam:** *Drishtānto drishtānta yukto Nidarshanam,* to clarify something with examples is called *Nidarshanam.*

22. **Apavargah:** *Abhipluta vyapakarshanam Apavargah,* to discuss the rules so much in detail that it dimnishes the subject, is called *Apavargah.*

23. **Swa-sangyā:** *Paraira sanmitah shabdah swa-sangyāI,* the word that is used without any directive from others is called *swa-sangyā.*

24. **Purva Pakshah:** *Pratishedhvyam vākyam purva pakshah;* the sentence that admonishes is called *Purva Paksha.*

25. **Uttar Pakshah:** *Tasya nirnayan vākyam uttar paksham;* that which denies the statement of *Purva Paksha* is called *Uttar Paksha.*

26. **Ekāntah:** *Sarva trāyatam Ekāntah;* that statement which can't be left out at any place or any time, is called *Ekāntah.*

27. **Anāgat Āvekshanam:** *Panchādevam vihitam itya Anāgat Āvekshanam,* the provision that has to be made in the future is called *Anāgat Āvekshanam.*

28. Atikrānta Āvekshanam: *Purastād yevam vihitam itya Atikrānta Āvekshanam*; the provision that has already been made is called *Pratikrānta Āvekshanam*.

29. Niyogah: *Yevam nānyath iti Niyogah*, the statement that says that this work is to be performed in this way or not at all, is called *Niyoga*.

30. Vikalpah: *Anena vānena veti Vikalpah*; the thing can be done either this way or that way, is called *Vikalpa*.

31. Samuchchyah: *Anena cha anena cha iti samuchchyah*; a thing that can be done in this way and that way, is called *Samuchchya*.

32. Uhyam: *Anukta karanam Uhyam*; to do what has not been said, is called *Uhya*.

In this way, Arth has 32 divisions and the *Artha Shāstram* by Kautilya deals with all these 32 ways and means:

Yevam shāstram idam yuktam yetābhih tantra yukti bhih;
Avāptau pālane cha uktam lokasyāsya parasya cha.

This Artha (and Arthshāstra) encourages one to indulge in Artha and Kāma, save them, and destroy opposition caused by non-religious activities:

Dharmam artham cha kāmam cha pravartayati pāti cha;
Adharma anarth vidveshān idam shāstram idam nihanti cha.

In the concluding lines (180th *Prakaran*) it is said that this Arthshāstra is written by that Vishnugupta Kautilya, who freed the land, weapons and scriptures from King Nand:

Yena shāstram cha shastram cha nand rāja gatā cha bhuh;
Amarshena udhritānya āshu tena shāstram idam kritam.

When *artha* is to be taken as one of the pursuits then it cannot be taken in its limited connotation, and only as the money or the wealth. As pursuit it must cover all. Moreover, mere accumulation of money is not *artha*; its best and most advantageous utilization is also allied with it. Money must be *ānand dāyakam; dharma dhārakam* and *Moksha kārkam:* money must give pleasure; keep morality intact and be a provision for liberation. If otherwise, then money is useless. We know, only a single way to use money: to buy things for food and luxury. This is not utilization at all, it is spending, expense. One must take it in its widest perspective.

Due to the broad attitude that Chānakya perceived and followed, he was successful in fulfilling his higher and almost unachievable dreams.

6

Destroying Old Order and Enemies

Uproot which Pinches

One famous incident from Chānakya's life proves how strong, inimical, intolerant he was; and how he yearned for the safety and obstacle-free path towards the goal. Perhaps he believed in demolishing dilapidated structure and old order for greater gain, better creation and smooth progress.

One day a kush (a kind of grass, with a sharp needle-like top, used in the religious observances by the Hindus) pricked Chanak's foot, the father of Chānakya. It became septic and eventually Chanak died. Chānkya did observe the rituals but he could neither forget nor forgive kush. He studied it, made preparations and started uprooting and annihilating the very species of kush by pouring whey at the broken roots of kush so that they may not germinate or grow again. This was his way of showing anger and taking vengeance.

The people were amazed to see it. A young man taking whey every morning and going out in search of kush, uprooting them and pouring at each root, a bit of whey to erase them was a sight to watch. Some of them didn't like it. They protested. It had no effect on the mind and action of the revengeful and determined Chānakya. One day, some elderly persons (In another version, one of the ministers of Nand, saw him uprooting kush and the brilliance on his face,) went to Chānakya who was busy in uprooting and destroying quite innocent looking but sharp needle-like kush. They politely asked, ``What and why are you doing?''

"I'm uprooting and destroying this pinching kush because I can't tolerate anything against man or humanity, and whosoever goes against man or humanity I'll destroy it."

He was true to his word. His body language expressed more than his words. The minister thought him to be the best person to go against Nand and destroy him. It was that Minister who invited him to a feast arranged by the king knowing well that Nand will not tolerate a black brāhmin and this brāhmin won't tolerate Nand. It will suit him. That way, Chānakya reached the palace.

He won't easily express his mind for he held the view one should not make their inner decisions known to others. He said, "manasā vichintyayet vachasā na prakāshayet."

At some places it's written that once he was going to some place with his disciples. He had taken an un-treaded route. He wore no protection for his feet. A kush pricked. It was painful. He immediately asked the pupils to bring whey, to uproot them and to pour whey at each root to abolish it completely. When other men asked him the reason of his anger he plainly replied that he can't tolerate any obstacle on his way. He further added that he liked to uproot whatever pinched.

Appraisal

It is almost impossible to ascend higher without creating enemies, and doubly difficult to ascend higher in the face of the enemies. Face the enemies wisely and at the right opportunity without losing a lot of time, energy or resources.

The Vow: Resolution and Aim

There are different versions of each incident associated with Chānakya. The writers have used their own imagination to paint the person, visualize his moves and express his ideas. This one is not an exception. Usually, it is said that Chānakya went to the court of Magadhnaresh Ghanānand on his own but another version says that because he was a scholar he was made the president of a charitable trust and met the king for the first time as the president of the said trust. But it can't be true that all such appointments were made directly by the king.

The most convincing tale is that he was invited by one of the ministers to attend a feast arranged by the king and when Nand saw him, he was angry and asked his men to throw the black brāhmin out of the court. This insult was such that Chānakya was too angry to be checked and took a vow to destroy the king and his clan.

There is yet another version that one minister from the court of the Magadhnaresh who was angry with him as he was insulted by the king, took Chānakya to the court. He knew something about Chānakya's background, power, and nature. He invited him to the court knowing well that the king will not tolerate his black face and arrogant ways. He will insult the Brāhmin and the Brāhmin will take the revenge. His aim will be fulfilled. He did exactly as he planned and truly enough, the luxuriant king forgot the courtesy to be shown towards a Brāhmin. Whatever the reason, Chānakya was in the court of King Ghanānand.

On the other hand Nand laughed at the black and ugly Brāhmin:

"Is he a Brāhmin? A Brāhmin can't be black and if black he can't be a Brāhmin." It had dual meanings.

Chānakya did not like the ways of the king. He protested but of no avail. The minister concerned was pleased with the expected turn in event. He sided with his king which angered Chānakya even more. The situation grew tense.

Many of them didn't like to insult a Brāhmin but Ghanānand was obstinate. He won't listen to reason. He loved luxury and was cruel to the people. He had brutally taxed the people to fill the treasure. People were annoyed. He was not popular among them. It was because of his temperament, character and behaviour.

Ghanānand started laughing at the Brāhmin who was fast losing his patience. He roared in the court against the king. In return the king ordered:

"Throw this Brāhmin out of the court."

It brought the end of the preserved patience. Chānkya broke loose. He showered verbal curses on the king and the kingdom. No one was

able to check them. In a fit of anger Ghanānand inflicted more injury. The angry Brāhmin freed himself from the grip of the soldiers, untied the sacred lock of hair at the crown of the head, and took a vow:

"Ghanānand, I have come to show you the true path and stop you from luxurious living, free you from surā and sunderi, wine and women, but you won't listen to reason. I take a vow in the presence of all that I will annihilate you and your dynasty. I won't take rest till you are not destroyed along with your posterity. I will not bind my choti (the lock of hair) till you are not uprooted."

Chānakya marched out of the court in that angry mood.

Appraisal

Don't make a promise but in case you make a promise then fulfill it in time and with the best ability. Don't take a vow but in case you take a vow then direct all your energy and resources to make your vow come true. That gives immense confidence and pleasure of being a winner.

Effect

We grow from inside. Our power comes from inside. The inner soul is all "energy". Enrich it for instant and greater success.

The Preparations

The king was not worried. After all, what could a feeble Brāhmin do to him? But Chānakya was restless. He could not forget the vow taken in the court, in the presence of the courtiers. His open lock of hair reminded him many times everyday rather whenever he touched it or whenever the air blew it. He had taken such a great vow which was obviously very difficult to fulfill. He lost his appetite, his sleep. He stopped thinking about anything else.

He had to arrange each and everything, from a simple needle to a sharp and heavy sword. This made him a tireless worker, busy almost the whole day and whole night and in-between taking a nap here and an hour's sleep there.

Establishing an Empire or Organization

Chānakya showed us the way how to get a vow come true by exterminating the Nanda Dynasty, who were the rulers of the Magadha Empire. The entire dynasty became traceless. It was a grand success for Chānakya. It is the only example of a strong empire being uprooted by an individual who had neither wealth nor army; neither a house nor a living; neither land nor residence; neither known people nor known resources; and neither weapons nor physical strength. That is why Chānakya declares that knowledge and wisdom is everything to get success.

The Birth of Arthashāstra

Though, the legendary work *Kautilya Arthashāstra* was written very late but Chānakya conceived the idea of the work while thinking about the infamous Magadha King Ghanānand and comparing him with a great and righteous king. It got its roots in his mind when he was planning the demolition of the Nand dynasty, and construction of a new empire, making preparations, acquiring material wealth, gaining in strength, raising an army, and training recruits. At that time he had both the ideas of destruction and construction running parallel in his mind.

He declared that the learned king who works for the welfare of all living beings and is always ready to do the best for the administration and education of the people rules over his kingdom for a long time:

Vidyā vinito rājā hi prajānām vinaye ratah;
Ananyām prithivim bhungagkte sarva bhuta hite ratah.

Vriddha Sanyogah

He can win any land and rule for a long time if one had won over the six enemies – sex, anger, lust, ego, pride, and jealousy (*kāma- krodha- lobha- mān- mad- aharsha tyāgāt kāryah*).

A king can't do anything singnificant as one wheel will not move the chariot. So, many helping hands are needed, *Sahāya asādhyam rājatvam chakram yekam na vartate.* For that purpose different persons suited for different jobs are to be appointed.

The *Arthashāstra* classifies legal matters into civil and criminal and it specifies elaborate guidelines for administering justice in terms of evidence, procedures and witnesses. Furthermore, Kautilya strongly believed in *Dandniti*, though he maintained that penalties must be fair and just, and proportionate to the offence committed. The people don't like the king who announces disproportionate tough punishments; they don't obey a lenient king, so it is better to give just and proportionate punishment,

Teekshna dando hi bhutānām udejaniya.
Mridu dandah paribhuyate.
Yathārtha dandah pujyah.

Vārtā- Danda- Niti- Sthāpanā

In *Arthashāstra*, 6000 verses, mainly prose with about 380 *shlokas*, have been divided into 15 *adhikaranas* (books) and 150 *adhyāyas* and 180 *prakaranas* (sections dealing with one topic). It begins with *Mulāni*-Foundations and *Mantrinah*-Counselors

In short it can be seen in this way:

Kāryam – Work	*Mantrinah-Kāryarthi-*
Rājya Tantram - Mangement	*Mantra*-Policies, Strategies
Kārya Siddhih – Work Accomplished	*Kāryārthi* – Work manager
	Juga Loka – Human relations
Rājya Neeti – Management Science	*Sandhi* – Alliances
	Arthakamau – Wealth and Desires
Sāhas – Managerial Actions	*Danda* - Enforcement
Ācharanam – Behaviour	*Charitram* – Character
Artha – Resources	*Utsāh* – Enthusisam, Entrepreneurship
Dosha – Faults	
Kāryavyāpti – Working	*Svajana* – Own people
Dharma – Ethics	

The Basic Factors

Kingdom or organization or an enterprise is the basis of resources. One person can earn enough but only for a family but if hundreds, or thousands or lakhs of people are working for a person who owns a kingdom or an enterprise then the profit earned by all the men after deducting their salary adds up to the resources of that man and hence, his earning multiplies hundreds of times. The resources are controlled, surplus generated and used for different purposes through the possession of a kingdom. Chānakya draws attention towards certain facts. The large nations states/ corporations today are similar in structure to kingdoms but are governed by elected/appointed representatives of the people/ stakeholders. The development of science, technology and engineering with the market economy has resulted in wealth generation through the industry and services sector. This is in addition to agriculture which has always existed.

The basis of enterprise is rooted in conquering the body organs

➤ Management of "everything" begins with management of "self".

- Management cannot be separated from the manager.
- *Indriya* or organs of sense – eyes, ears, nose, tongue, and skin.
- Organs of action: Hands, feet, mouth, reproduction, and excretion.
- Organ of perception: Mind
- Manifestation of *indriya jaya*: Control over: *kāma, krodha, lobha, moha, mada* and *matsarya*.
- *Indriyajayasya mulam vinayam*: The conquest of the organs lies in training/discipline.
- Mastery of the self lies in the self; discipline/humility generated by training in ethics.
- *Virupasevanam vigyānam*: Worldly knowledge is learned from serving the elders.
- *Vigyānam*: Sciences and art; human behaviour.
- *Gyānam*: Spiritual/philosophical knowledge.
- *Vijnanaena atmamanam sampādyet*: Equip yourself fully with worldly knowledge; enrich yourself internally; cognitive acquisition of worldly knowledge followed by internalization leading to appropriate behaviour, in practise lead to better performance at tasks undertaken.
- *Sampaditātma jitātma bhavati*: One who has acquired knowledge is the one who has conquered himself. Totally self-controlled professional leader/manager acts in the long-term interest of the organization; resists acting in self interest which conflicts with organizational interest; does not succumb to pressure of immediate interests against long-term interests; resists temptations to do good to the organization at the cost of society,

nations and stakeholders; prepared to quit rather make decisions against convictions.

➤ *Jitātmā Sarvarthe sanyujyate*: The self-conquered should endow himself with all resources.

➤ *Sarvarthe:* All resources: Men; Money; Materials; Methods.

7

The Last Blow

After worldly knowledge is acquired, resources do not come on their own. They have to be deliberately acquired in order to be victorious in all tasks undertaken and enterprise building. These are parts of the preparation for the final blow to the opposition and for blowing the victory bugle.

From day one, Chānakya kept on thinking and planning the final blow to Nand dynasty. He rescheduled his plans and started attacking the border areas where the king would take time to reach, giving easier success to the declared enemy. But Chānakya was not satisfied with the border areas. He had taken the vow to uproot the king, Purna vināsham vadāmi.

Chānakya had started placing and establishing his own men in Pātaliputra and the palace. He did not follow only the prescribed four ancient ways of Sāma, Dāma, Danda and Bheda but added three more of his own and followed them all as the preparation for the final blow. He treated all the persons who were insulted at the hands of the arrogant king or were angry with him as his friend and supporters. Whenever needed, he met them or sent messages. Inside the capital city and the palace he created and placed an assorted army for different purposes. He had bought together not only the army men and officials, ministers and influential Vaishyas but even prostitutes and their men.

He knew that most of the royal figures, ministers and officers were regular visitors of prostitutes. It was easier for him to mix intoxicants in the wine supplied to them. It did the trick. No one ever suspected

that the wine that they were taking had intoxicants. Secrecy was maintained painstakingly.

His numerous secret agents were doing their level best to take away one pillar after another to weaken the palace so that it could tumble down with one powerful thrust. It happened exactly in that way.

When all the necessary preparations were made, then one auspicious day, Chānakya came to Pātliputra with all the strength that he had mustered up. He placed them intelligently and covered all the key posts and points. His men were following the instructions to the letter.

Just after midnight, the whole of the small Mauryan army attacked the capital city and before the officials realized what was happening, they entered the palace. Most of the officials and higher authorities were captured and imprisoned from the kothās, residences cum work places of the prostitutes in an intoxicated state.

King Ghanānand was caught playing with selected young women. He was readily imprisoned in a half-naked state. Within hours and *without bloodshed, all the royal persons and the king were imprisoned and the Nand dynasty was completely uprooted.*

In the early hours of the morning of that colossal change, Chānakya took a bath, performed poojā and ceremoniously intertwined and bound his plait; the lock of hair at the crown of head that he had loosened in the court of the king Nand. It was done at the same spot where he had opened it while taking a vow. The last blow was successful and the vow was accomplished.

The Sun was brighter and happier that day.

Appraisal

One can't get that satisfaction which comes from small or big accomplishment as all our efforts are directed towards some accomplishment. That is final or ultimate which comes repeatedly in the life of a successful man and his life becomes a cluster of many finals won. Work with zeal and make concentrated effort to win all the finals that come your way.

Effect

The total gain is important. There is no doubt about it. But honest, concentrated effort is more valuable than all the gains which are the by-products of the effort.

Perfected Theory on Experiences

➤ The people of the town and cities would never survive without the works, production and system of the countryside. So, it is clear that the road to wealth, health and prosperity goes by the countryside.

➤ Only a balanced wage system can keep the balance in life, production and distribution while the modern system claims that the wages should not be fixed but negotiated and experts from the rival company or country should be bought at a higher salary. This way the loyalty also shifts which weakens the employees and they even lose faith. There are employees that get as low as two thousand per month and as high as two crores per month.

> Right kind of employees should be selected and given right training in such a way that they never feel bored with their nature of work. This way, they won't face stress, depression and strain. Among them, there should be right leaders or managers. The other employees will grow under a mentor.

> The employees must be motivated; they must know their powers and responsibilities. The powers and duties must be well-defined among the employees of different cadre taken for different purposes.

> Correct information must be easily passed in right urgency. The shirkers must be known and punished adequately: socially, psychologically and financially. Financial punishment is the weakest punishment. Before punishment, corrective measures should be taken. It will increase alertness.

> There must be a correct and effective strategy to face and defeat the opponents, competitors or kings.

> There must be a robust and correct internal accounting system so that no one can raise a finger against the payment or non-payment.

> Chānkaya or Kautilya or Vishnu Sharmā had very good advice for the entrepreneurs. They should never be in dilemma whether to venture it or not. They should be ethical and take needed training before venturing into a new project. After all, they are the bosses, they have to manage and control. Only that way, they can reach and stay at the top.

- Command but do not demand promotion in the job. Protect against all sorts of enemies: internal and external. Knowledge and training of a leader plays an important role. Correct, timely and profitable decision making, makes a leader.
- Pay your taxes in time to avoid complications.
- Don't opt for multiple projects. Get specialization. Never depend only on borrowed specialists.
- Kautilya lays stress on continuous learning of the king, the director or the chief executive and that of the workers.
- One can change job if one has acquired greater knowledge and skill but not for only money.
- If someone dies on duty then the employer should look after his family.
- Grab the right opportunity.
- Be an asset never a burden; be savior not a threat.
- Don't corrupt uncorrupt mind.
- The winner's sharpest weapon is secrecy.
- Don't worry about loss, multiply the gain.
- Be the strongest pillar but never a weak link.
- Manage the self to know how to manage others.

Chānakya had followed these methods and got success, so he mentioned all these things in his grand treatise. Of course, it had already taken a lot of time than what he desired but finally he succeeded in completely destroying Magadhnaresh and his Nand dynasty. It also took time since the aim was destruction of one and establishment of another powerful dyanasty.

8

Making of a King: the Chief

Chānakya was a learned man, a practical thinker, a proud Brāhmin, a conscious executive and an immaculate planner. He had taken the vow to completely destroy the Nand dynasty. His loosened the long and thick central lock behind his head that always reminded him that the vow is still to be fulfilled. He had the required plan to generate resources and raise an army to do the needful. He knew that he was not a warrior; that he was able to carry the books, not the sword; that he was a strategist, not a killer. He could lead an army from behind but he couldn't lead from the front. He needed a brave soldier, a lenient man, a disciplined disciple, a wise, strong and handsome youth, and a person who could mix with all without losing his individual status. He knew only such a person could fulfill his dreams, could execute his plans, change his ideas into reality and ascend the peak. He was looking for such a brilliant boy. Luck was on his side.

Search for the Future King

Chānakya established a hermitage where he started teaching the young students whom he wanted to train as soldiers and commanders. But whosoever was there with him, there was no one who showed the potential to be the king. So, Chānakya planned to move from village to village for material wealth to feed the students and to acquire weapons both for training and for the army to be raised; to recruit more and more young men to raise a big and expert army and to search for a "new king".

One day, in the plains of the Ganga, in a rich looking village full of greenery, he saw cows and cowboys. He was attracted to a tall boy who held his head high and was standing on a big stone. He was looking at the cattle and directing the boys. He was posing to be the king. Chānakya was engrossed in the drama. The boy sat on the stone as if it was the throne. He sent many boys as messengers and soldiers to do the tit-bits. When the boy saw Chānakya, he called him and when Chānakya approached him he asked:

"What do you want Learned Brāhmin?" The boy knew how to honour a Brāhmin.

Chānakya humbly replied, "I need cows to feed my pupils with milk."

The boy knew the value of charity. Without any hesitation he ordered, "This learned Brāhmin should be given one hundred and one cows."

Chānakya bowed humbly and asked, "Have you taken permission from your guardians?"

"A king does not need to take permission from others." The boy knew the powers of a king and was sure that he was doing something good. One must be charitable.

In the same mood Chānakya asked "Where are your parents?"

The boy directed his index finger towards the village. Chānakya

had already read the forehead and now he got the opportunity to read the palm. He saw what he wished to see. Now he was listening to the boy more intently.

The boy said, "I've no father. My mother lives there." The boy longed for the place.

"And what's the name of your mother." Chānakya wanted to know more.

"Mātā Murā" was the emotional reply.

"Victory to the king! I will come back to take the cows." Chānakya blessed the boy and turned towards the village.

He met the mother of the boy. The boy also joined them. He wanted to take the boy to make him a king. She was not willing to part with the only child she had. The boy was on the mother's side. Chānakya spent the whole evening and the whole night convincing them. The next morning was a bright morning. Chānakya took the boy and returned to his newly-established hermitage to educate and train him with the other young boys who were already taking training. In his eyes, they were the future soldiers, commanders, officials and ministers.

The boy was baptized. He was given a new name, Chandragupta, to which the name of his mother Mura was added as Maurya.

Appraisal

Painstaking and wise selection reduces the burden and tension. If manpower is not powerful and active then a lot is required to be done but with skillful and diligent manpower the expenses and time are drastically cut down.

Effect

Select the best and be relaxed; select the ordinary and remain always in doubt.

The training of the future king started. He planned everything meticulously for the boy from what to eat and what not; what to read and what not; from whom to meet and what to say to what not to say and whom to ignore. He prepared for him a routine and among the trainees he was declared the king so that he can imbibe the great qualities of a great and righteous future king.

Chānakya proved true to his words. He made him the king, Chandragupta Maurya, and started the Maurya dynasty, a great dynasty and that period is considered to be the golden period in ancient Indian history, but it took many years.

The village was Pippali Kānan, full of mango orchards in the Champakāranya. It was here that Rama stayed for two days while returning from Janakpur after the marriage with Sita. A pond was dug there which is known as "Sita Kunda". The mango grove is still there and there are two small temples: Shiva Temple and Rama Temple. It is some 120 kilometers from Patliputra in the north. After becoming the Minister and establishing the Maurya dynasty, Chānakya used to live here. He had special fascination for the place. Though his Fort, known as Chānaki Garha, is about 120 kilometers in the west from there in Narkatiaganj.

An Organization: An Empire
Relevance of the *Arthashāstra* in present times:
Chānakya knew that one or two things won't give him success and fulfill his dreams, so he was conscious of many things. Yet, he did not ignore his studies. He kept on reading the great treatises that he painstakingly collected. In the *Kautilya Arthashāstra*, at many places, Chānakya has mentioned many scholars who have given their ideas regarding the administration of an empire. Chānakya has opposed some views, explained many and accepted a few. It is enough to indicate that there were other works and treatises on the topic but there is none alive. It is the timelessness and agelessness of Chānakya's *Arthashāstra* that

it is still alive and effective like its creator, the legendary and immortal figure who single-handedly changed the course of time and history of a nation divided in many small kingdoms.

People, even experts, usually think and say that whatever Chānakya has written in the *Arthashāstra* deals with the management of an empire and it is related to the powers and duties and training, etc., of an emperor. That is the difference between that time and modern time. Due to western influence all the kingdoms and empires have changed into Business Houses and Business Empires, the king and ministers and persons on different posts have changed into Managing Directors, Directors, and Executives on different scales and in different milieu. The portfolios have changed, the designations have changed but the responsibilities, duties, and powers have remained the same. There lies the similarity and if it is seen, read and understood in this light then the *Arthashāstra* is a superb book and has no peer.

If one asks: "Is this book, i.e the *Arthashāstra* written over thousands of years ago still applicable in today's world?"

The answer is ready for such a man: "Yes it is, because the *Arthashāstra* is a book about the management of the "living beings"; "life at large"; "human mind"; "human life"; "trade" and "natural resources", which has not changed a lot and the basics have remained the same since ages: both the resources and the work except heavy intrusion of machine which has created an army of unemployed persons in every country across the world. *So as long as the human mind remains filled with its negativities of jealousy, ego, hatred and over indulgence, so long as human beings require self control, discipline and management., 'Kautilaya's Arthashāstra will remain relevant.*

Chānakya in his world-famous book *Kautilya's Arthashāstra* has brought out some of the key business principles and strategies. Apart from the scholarly work, this book needs to be once again represented for practical application in today's world. The book has got many principles and techniques, and by applying thses we can bring tremendous improvements even in our day-to-day management.

An organization is definitely like an empire and the Managing Director or the Chief is the emperor that has an army of expert employees and workers and its complete marketing area its boundary or frontiers. The consumers of its products are the citizens that pay taxes in the form of profit. Many collaborators, dealers, sole distributors are friends and organizations in similar business are competitors, like enemies.

Everything that Kautilya has thought and said is for the safety, peace, prosperity and happiness of the state, such organizations, its directors and of its subject; both employees and users. His advice is not against any of the two: the ruler and the ruled; the master and the servant; or the employer and the employee.

Leadership Qualities

In an organization and in management, the leader rules and hence, leadership qualities are enhanced. Leadership is the ability to persuade others to seek predefined objectives enthusiastically is one part of the truth; the other part is that the leader must be wise enough to guide others whenever needed. There is no limitation of work and field. Those that lack leadership qualities are now starting virtual organizations and such virtual organizations are farce, and planned and created to mislead others. One must have that power as one has the authority and authority is the power and hence, needs power to utilize discretion in making decisions to be followed by others. Lack of wisdom and deviations create problems.

An organization is an institution for peace and prosperity. Its division in formal and Informal has nothing to do with its functioning. Both originate from work on similar patterns: deliberate or spontaneous. Its policies declare the ways the company is to deal with stakeholders, employees, customers, suppliers, distributors and other important and allied groups. In comparison to traditional business modern business organizations are unhealthy, feeble, vulnerable, instable and dependent while they vociferously claim the opposite.

Economic growth and the growth of business and business community can't be possible without the active cooperation and participation of non-business community.

It's in the long run and enlightened interest of corporations and commercial organizations to promote public welfare in a positive way, as they are capable of fighting and solving any social problem efficiently and effectively. A company growing and moving for diversification may need an entrepreneurial top management, while a large and well-established company may require more professionalism in management. The socio-cultural environment that consists of attitudes, beliefs, desires, expectations and customs of the society, determines the production, its distribution, price and even profit.

Effective and able managers must possess the following personal characteristics: decisive; aggressive; amiable; conforming; self-starting; productive; well informed; determined; energetic; creative; intelligent; responsible; enterprising; and clear thinking.

The principles of management are: to increase efficiency; to crystallize the nature of management; to carry on researches and to attain social objectives. There are some other very good principles for better management:

> ➤ Employ only the best, even on premium, at the key posts. It's the character, integration and sacrifice of the employees that make the difference. Depression in life and management is caused by lack of faith.

> ➤ Attend to your mails, get appreciated and accepted; throw your mails to dustbin, get rejected and thrown out from adorning eyes.

- It is easy to save own or others' money; it is difficult to save words and character. Those are happy that save.
- Complete each new work in a bit better way than the previous one. You will automatically grow better.
- Work for work, for pleasure, for honour, respect or all of them combined together but never work for money alone.
- Don't visit the places where you don't get respect, don't meet the persons who have no sense of propriety. Those persons are honourable that have life inside and God overhead.
- Don't allow doubt to creep into mind, keep faith and be faithful.
- If you want to win, win over your lust; if you want to grow, help others. The more you help the more help you get.
- Satisfaction is a boon and work is a blessing.
- Weigh the words that you say; not the money that you pay.
- If you live possessing or possessed by the universe your death is divine.
- Always do good you won't see bad days. Take a weapon swords will come out against you.
- Sleep after work; not during work.

An ideal king is one who has the highest qualities of leadership, intellect, energy and personal attributes.

The qualities of Leadership which attract followers and give success:

- Birth in a noble family
- Good fortune
- Intellect and prowess

- Association with elders
- Righteousness
- Truthfulness
- Resolute
- Enthusiastic
- Disciplined
- Honours promises
- Gratitude and gratefulness
- Lofty aims
- Not being dilatory
- Stronger than neighbouring kings/competitors and
- Possess ministers of high quality

The qualities in an Intellectual king
- Desire to learn
- Listening (to others)
- Grasping, retaining
- Understanding thoroughly and reflecting on knowledge
- Rejecting false views and adhering to the true ones

An energetic king is one who is
- Valorous
- Determined
- Quick, and
- Dexterous

An ideal king should be
- Eloquent
- Bold and endowed with sharp intellect

- Possess strong memory and a keen mind
- Amenable to guidance
- Well trained in all the arts and
- Be able to lead the army
- Be just in rewarding and punishing
- He should have the foresight to avail himself of the opportunities (by choosing) the right time, place and type of action.
- He should know how to govern in normal times and in times of crisis
- He should know when to fight and when to make peace, when to observe treaties and when to strike at an enemy's weakness.
- He should preserve his dignity at all times and not laugh in an undignified manner
- He should be sweet in speech, look straight at people and avoid frowning
- He should eschew passion, anger, greed, obstinacy, fickleness and backbiting
- He should conduct himself in accordance with the advice of elders

The Rājarishi: Guide Lines

The *Arthashāstra* deals in detail with the qualities and disciplines required for Rājarishi, a wise and virtuous king. With wise moves, patient teaching, continuous training and unmatched alertness Chānakya put all the great qualities in his new disciple and the future king Chandraguta Maurya. He has expressed those qualities in the *Arthashāstra*. One thing more, it is evident from his writings that he was not looking only for a simple replacement for the existing king but wanted to establish a righteous dynasty for a long time. So, he was not satisfied with the general qualities of a king but wanted to put in the higher and exceptional qualities too. He has declared:

"The king's happiness lies in the happiness of his subjects, their welfare is his welfare. He shall not consider as good only that which pleases him but treat as beneficial to him whatever pleases his subjects."

According to Kautilya, a Rājarshi is one who:

> Has self-control, having conquered the inimical temptations of the senses
> Cultivates the intellect by association with elders
> Keeps his eyes open through spies
> Is ever active in promoting the security & welfare of the people
> Ensures the observance by the people of their *dharma* by authority and example
> Improves his own discipline by continuous learning in all branches of knowledge
> Endears himself to his people by enriching them and doing good to them

Such a disciplined king should

> Keep away from another's wife;
> Not covet another's property;
> Practise *ahimsā*, non-violence towards all living beings
> Avoid day dreaming, capriciousness, falsehood and extravagance; and
> Avoid association with harmful persons and indulging in (harmful) activities.

Higher and Exceptional Qualities of a disciplined King

Abhigāmika Guna: Sublime family tradition; divine intelligence; embodiment of patience; farsightedness; Righteous; truthfully true; true to words and promises; gratefulness; highly ambitious; passionately enthusiastic; fast accomplishing ability; enchanting; determined and versed in scriptures.

Pragyā Guna: Knowledge of Scriptures; Discussions on Scriptures; minute receptivity; tenacious and retentive memory; specialization on known subjects; to draw deepest meaning through logical thinking and questioning; discard and disregard negativity; graciously accepting positive and rare qualities.

Utasāh Guna: Valour and bravery; intolerant and wrathful; nimbleness and oscillation; dexterity and efficiency.

Ātma Sampanna: Confident and resolute; mature and bold; impertinent and insolent; energetic and active; impudent and haughty; exceptional memory; excessive powerful; magnanimous; controlled and balanced; expert rider; saviour in calamity; benevolent; shy of asking; deep insight and far sight; wise and diligent in fight; enriching coffin without inflicting injury; pleasant; soft and sweet spoken; honour and respect for old and wise.

Qualities of **Township, Fort, Treasure, Army, Friends, Enemies**; have been discussed and given keeping very fine details in mind.

Duties of the King

If the king is energetic, his subjects will be equally energetic. If he is slack and lazy in performing his duties, the subjects will also be lax and thereby eat into his wealth. Besides, a lazy king easily falls into the hands of enemies. Hence, the Mahārāja should always be energetic. He shall divide the day and the night, each into eight periods of one and half hours, and perform his duties as follows:

Engagements in the Morning
➤ Receive reports on defence, revenue and expenditure
➤ Public audiences, to hear petitions of the city and country people

> Receive revenues and tributes; appoint ministers and other high officials and assign tasks to them

Engagements during Noon Hours

> Write letters and dispatches, confer with councillors
> Receive secret information from spies
> Personal: recreation, time for contemplation

Engagements during Evening Hours

> Personal: bath, meals, study
> Inspect review forces; Consult with the Chief of Defence

Engagements after Sunset

> Counseling with the secret agents
> Retire to the bed chamber to the sound of music, sleep

Engagements after Midnight

> Meditate on political matters and on work to be done
> Consult with councilors, send out spies

Engagements before Sunrise

> Religious, household and personal duties.

Meetings with his teacher, adviser on rituals, purohitas, personal physician, chief cooks and astrologer should be held regularly. A king or a chief can follow this or some other time table which suits him. Under his training, Chandragupta had to follow the routine irrespective of whether Chānakya was present in the hermitage or not. The result was that he started looking after and controlling the hermitage on the prescribed pattern without minute to minute interference and advice of his learned teacher.

The king/director or the chief shall be ever active in the management of the economy. The root of wealth is activity and lack of it brings material distress. In the absence of fruitful economic activity, both current prosperity and future growth will be destroyed. A king can achieve the desired objectives and abundance of riches by undertaking (productive) economic activity.

Birth of a Prince: An Heir

With Chandragupta in the forefront, Chānakya demolished the Nand dynasty and established the Maurya dynasty. Many smaller kingdoms and the living relatives and friends of King Ghanānad could not digest this; rather they hated both Chānakya and Chandragupta. They were always busy in conspiring to kill them. Chandragupta was under constant threat and vulnerable too. He did not realize the danger but Chānakya knew it and was conscious about the safety of the emperor. Only he knew what had he done to select, prepare and train a righteous and powerful king for the country.

He was unable to control the thoughts of the friends of Nand or the lust of his relatives. They were getting a lot of money and an opportunity to lead a luxurious life without doing much. The new king declared end of luxury to them. So, they were attempting to kill the emperor.

Once, a guptachar (spy) of another kingdom, disguised as an envoy, came to meet Chandragupta. Chānakya was suspicious. His secret agents gave him the feedback and true identity of the spy and his intention to kill the emperor. *The meeting was arranged. The envoy went inside to meet him but an alert Chānakya kept an eye on them from behind the curtain with his own men ready for action.*

Though the two were alone but three others were watching them. The envoy talked of the sweet sorbet of his country and offered a bottle. He prepared two glasses of sorbet and handed over one to Chandragupta. When the king was about to drink it, Chānakya dramatically came out from behind the curtain, stopped Chandragupta from taking the drink and ordered the arrest and death of the secret agent.

Chandragupta was stunned while Chānakya showed impeccable outer patience while he was boiling with anger from inside. His anxiety about the king and restless for his safety grew.

This was one stray incident but five more followed in a short span of time. Chānakya knew that the there is no end to the conspiracy towards a ruler. Then the only remedy is the strength of the ruler. He was assured of Chandragupta's physical strength, war acumen, and winning ability. None could defeat him but he was worried about the deceptive moves. Chandragupta seldom had doubt about the integrity of others.

Worried and able Chānakya decided to make the emperor's systems immune towards poison. He started administering a little poison in every meal to Chandragupta. It was done secretly by the chief royal cook. It went on for years. As Chānakya was an expert of medicines and poisons so he knew the fatal doze and healthy doze. He would himself prepare different kinds of poisons for the king.

Three queens were married to Chandragupta in separate ceremonies. They were Helen, Durdha and Chitrā. The second Queen Durdha was in the ninth month of pregnancy when a deadly incident occurred. The queen was weak and carrying a child. Chandragupta tried to give more time to her. They were expecting the son, the prince and heir of the Maurya Empire. He cared a lot about the queen.

The usual meal was served to the king with a bit of poison. Out of love and care, the king invited the queen to share the meal. The cook lost his wit. In place of stopping them on this or that ground or pretext, he ran up to Chānakya to inform. Chānakya rushed towards them.

In the meantime, the queen had taken a few morsels of the king's food. Her tender body and system could not digest it. It was late when Chānakya reached there. The queen was losing her consciousness. He wanted the heir and was worried about the poison passing on to the foetus. It would ruin everything.

Chānakya could not wait for the Vaidyas to administer medicines. Seconds were precious. Time was passing swiftly. At that moment, conscious Chānakya opted for surgery. In that very room, he operated upon the queen and took out the child from her womb. He saved the heir but could not save the queen who died because of the poison and the profuse blood that oozed out during the operation.

Chānakya may have read and known about surgery but it needs a lot of practise to operate on a person. He lacked that practise. It was his steady mind and grand memory that saved the heir but it was the mistake that took the life of the queen.

The foetus had taken a bindu (drop) of visha, (poison), the negative essence of plants, so he was named Bindusār. Chānakya fostered and trained the Prince. Bindusār was made the crown prince first, then the king of the great Maurya Empire in the lifetime of both Chandragupta and Chānakya. He too revered Chānakya and followed his advice to rule well over Greater India.

Appraisal

Patience is the hidden but constantly working power of a person. Only with patience one can keep a watch; learn and analyze the inside information and take timely, needed and correct action to get the desired result. The greater the patience, the greater is the success.

Training of a Future King

Chānakya knew and believed in the importance of self-discipline. Discipline is of two kinds – inborn and acquired. There must be an innate capacity for self-discipline for the reasons given below. Instruction and training can promote discipline only in a person capable of benefiting from them; people incapable of natural self-discipline are not benefited. Learning imparts discipline only to those who have the following mental facilities:

> ➤ Obedience to a teacher

> ➤ Desire and ability to learn

> ➤ Capacity to retain what is learnt

> ➤ Understanding what is learnt

> ➤ Reflecting on acquired knowledge

> ➤ Ability to make inferences by deliberating on facts

Those who are devoid of such mental faculties are not benefited by any amount of training. One who will be a king should acquire discipline and follow it strictly in life by learning the sciences from authoritative teachers.

The Training of a Prince

With improving self-discipline, the prince should always associate with learned elders, for in them alone has discipline its firm roots. For a trained intellect ensues yoga, successful application, from yoga comes self-possession. This is what is meant by efficiency in acquiring knowledge. Only that king will enjoy the earth unopposed who is wise, disciplined, devoted to a just governance of the subjects and conscious of the welfare of all beings.

Before the change and establishment of the Maurya dynasty, Chānakya trained Chandragupta and after the establishment he trained Prince Bindusār also. He did not live a relaxed life. For one who wishes to create and govern a large and great organization there is no free and relaxed moment. His pupils knew it, and followed the dictates of their teacher sincerely.

Enemy of an Enemy is a Friend

Magadha King Ghanānad was not a wise and strong ruler. He was arrogant and lascivious. Both his people and employees were against him but because of his known cruelty no one had the guts to speak openly against him. In his arrogance, the king forgot his duties and responsibilities and even the fact that people make a kingdom and people can give a throne or dethrone a king. Chānakya must have known it. He must have seen with his own eyes on his long way from south to the northeast of the vast country. When they learnt of the enmity of Chānakya, his open declaration of the ruin of the Nand dynasty, and about his hot preparations against him, they stood behind him without coming into the open. Chānakya declared it very late in his book but the people followed the concept that the *enemy of an enemy is a friend.*

It was just a chance that one day, Vaishyas, Pandas and rich farmers from the Gayā Region, a pilgrim centre; Mithilā Region and Vaishāli region came separately to meet him. Chānakya had some prior information because his espionage system, though small yet was on the track and working smoothly. Wherever he had gone, he had made friends and without appointing them as Guptachar, had given them the responsibility of Guptachars in his own effective way. Since, he had inkling into what was happening and who were eager to meet him so, he created the circumstance that they reached there on the same day. Perhaps, he wanted to prove to them that he

had the unconditional support of many from different regions. He did it cleverly.

Chānakya preferred to talk to the men from the Gayā Anchal as it was closer to Patliputra and had greater influence on the state of affairs. People from Vaishāli were closer and Mithila too were not far away but they had, in fact, no say in the political upheavals. They were peaceful and liked to live their life in their own way, which was of late disturbed.

He went up to the door of the largest hut in the hermitage to welcome the visitors. The leader introduced himself as Abhoy Shroff, a traditional goldsmith by profession. The others were not named though Chānakya knew the contingent but he did not mention it.

They placed their problems and concluded:

"We are ready to sacrifice for the health, prosperity and peace in the region. We are suffering in stead of living."

"It is too early to enter into a treaty but it's the word of a teacher that you will get the best deal when Chandra Maurya comes to throne. Both agriculture and business will be taken care of. The forests will yield and the rivers will irrigate more. People will be safe and satisfied," Chānakya clarified and gave confidence.

"In expectation of that return, we will manufacture and supply weapons along with expert and young men and regular and adequate material," they assured.

"Governance is all about security, safety and growth, which will be ensured. It is not an assurance, it is a fact. From tomorrow onwards, the Māgadhi Soldiers or officers will not come to you." Chānakya declared.

"How can it be possible?" They expressed their doubt.

"Four main officers in your area were killed last night. Both the ways leading to your area are under surveillance and protected, rather sealed. No army will be allowed to pass through those main routes. Your men are making preparation to take their charge today." Chānakya opened some secrets that his fistful daring soldiers had performed to take the full and unconditional support of the people.

"You are working fast. It's an excellent job." They praised with great relief as they usually prayed to be free from the four notorious persons of the area who were very close to the king and controlled everything. They checked their pleasure which was fast turning into ecstasy, ready to hear more.

"Not only I but all are busy performing their duties. A country is not safe if its people are not safe."Chānakya showed his confidence.

"We have some loaded carts with us. Please accept and treat it as the first of its kind." They stood up to take leave.

Later on, Chānakya met the other groups and the talk was almost similar with similar result. This sort of attitude of the people never allowed Chānakya to feel shortage of man, money and material as he managed the three meticulously well. It proved to be the basis of his tremendous success.

Fortunately for him, the time was ripe for revolt and the anger of the mass had started overflowing. Simply because of their support, his and the movements of the Maurya Army was not reported in time for officials to react and act.

Chānakya knew that people had the power and both Nand's people and personnel were against him ready to shift their loyalty. He has discussed these aspects in his book in detail. Moreover, he knew the value of small places, scattered hands and its honest and diligent people.

The Power of People or Employees

Although, Chānakya kept everyone under surveillance but he had empowered the employees of the Maurya dynasty. Of course, they were not allowed to act arbitrarily or do wrong but they possessed immense power, and had the authority to question anyone.

In modern context "employee empowerment" is not only a management buzzword but the employees and employers are coming closer and working hand in glove as they know that their survival depends on the success of the organization, and the success of an organization depends on the combined power and effort of the employees and the employers.

The employees are being given greater power and full accountability for the results, as they own the total responsibility of the work. That way the employees are being motivated and actually, they feel motivated and try their best to fulfill the responsibility. Their latent abilities are also utilized in a positive and constructive way. That is a sort of initiative and encourages an employee to perform his/her very best. Naturally, the employees should be given the liberty to perform their role to perfection to the extent their personal ability permits. This gives a lot of advantage to the organization. The organizers are sure and confident of the accomplishments of the given targets because they know that their employees are giving their best.

Employee empowerment adds to their positive thinking, approach and productivity. They feel that they are recognized and appreciated. The organization that does not give power to its employees suffers on many counts. They invariably run a race against time, because either they unnecessarily waste time talking to the immediate Boss for instruction or rushing to the head. It slows down the productivity. The employees lack self motivation and personal participation.

Modern executives too agree now that by giving employees paradigm to take decisions pertaining to their team, the customers and the work environment are bound to help them execute their role better and for greater advantage of the organization. The employees get a freehand to operate and take independent decision in the best interest of the organization and its employees. Naturally; they are all the time on their toes looking for something that needs immediate attention.

This gives an employee a sense of ownership, clarity in objectives and role that makes him/her more focused and goal-oriented. They prepare themselves for the next customer, next day, next month and thus for future. It gives job satisfaction and builds confidence. Such free yet dedicated employees, like Chānakya and his employees will always be assets. Anyway, one must feel responsible for the results, for own actions and the actions of the subordinates and show one's best "always".

Shifting Loyalty: Changing Organization

It is not that Chānakya had no idea and information about changing an organization for better and higher opportunity or when one disliked the chief, or when the chief was angry or when there were some disputes. In 4:93:5, entitled "Samaya Āchārikam" behaviour according to time and need Chānakya has given more than half a dozen examples when on trivial-looking incident the ministers left their kings:

➤ *Ayam uchaih: sinchititi Kātyāyanah pravavrāja.* The King said, "The labourer is irrigating from above." His Minister Kātyāyana left him.

➤ *Kraucha upasavyam iti Karniko Bhārdwājah.* The Krauch has flown from the left side. Heard Karnika from Bhārdwāja Gotra and left his king.

➤ *Trinam iti Deeraghah Chārāyana.* Āchārya Deergha Chārāyana left his king after looking at a straw.

➤ *Sheetā shātiti ghotamukhah.* Āchārya Ghota Mukha left his king when he heard him saying, "The clothe is cold".

➤ *Hasti pratyaukshiditi Kinjalkah.* The Minister named Kinjalka left his king when he saw him pouring water on the back of an elephant.

➤ *Rathāshwa prāshansiditi Pishunah.* Āchrya Pishuna left his king when he heard him praising the horse of the chariot.

➤ *Prati ravane shunah pishunputrah iti.* The son of that Pishuna left his king when he saw a dog barking at him.

Despite the above eye opening examples, Chānakya was always against shifting loyalty. The monetary gain may be far more than the expectations yet Chānakya won't allow or advise anyone to hop up or switch over to another organization. The person hopping now and then, and shifting loyalty from one company to another loses creditability. Chānakya could have accepted anything but not any weakness in character and determination. Once one accepted the job, he took some responsibility and some wages. He knew the conditions. In the meantime some changes took place, in all probability that "one" person got experience and grew from inside. Now he is more skilled, better equipped and possesses greater ability. It may be worth more than what salary he is getting from the place. So, he tries and gets a better placement or some other company shows interest and tries to buy the man on higher salary. If the person denies the offer and remains with the parent organization, he shows character and confidence and is later on rewarded by holding a key and more responsible post but if he switches over to another company, he would get the agreed salary but he could never win the confidence in the 2nd company, and will never be given any key post. Chānakya had that in mind when he said:

Tatra astho dosha nirghātam mitraih bhartari cha ācharet;
Tato bhartari jived wā mrite wā punah ābrajet.

(If there is some dispute or complain or anger, an employee should remain in the service of the master and clarify the situation through his friends or dear ones, and please him. One can leave that service when the original master dies.)

Nowadays, several employees, in quest to boost up their career prospects, resort to job hunting and hopping often without thinking about its pros and cons. They think, at present professional growth is only possible if one looks out for better options, and periodically change the organization that one works for.

That is also a reason that the companies are bent upon paying a meager starting salary as they know that the person would switch to some other company the moment he learns the tricks of the trade and gets adequate experience. They don't believe in them.

Some modern experts are also thinking in the line of Chānakya, "Changing job frequently reflects badly on one's resilience and loyalty to one's firm. If one is not loyal to one how can he/ she be expected to be loyal to others."

The following negative qualities come out to the fore: lower motivational level, and restlessness and lack of direction, and immature approach to a workplace.

In the interviews their commitment and loyalty to their previous employer are questioned. One question is very common, "Why do you want to leave them?"

It is double-edged hidden knife. If you show your own weakness your chances of getting the job become dim, and if you blame the parent company and if they happen to know the organizers of the company then you are labeled as a liar. You neither possess a definite philosophy nor have clear vision of your career goal.

Other questions follow closely. Some about the past experience and talent; the required job skills; fit to the concerned job profile and eye-brows are raised on the character, integrity, sense of responsibility and ability to do justice to the new post and organization. Believe it or not but a job-hopper's resume is always scrutinized minutely by recruiters and perspective employers. Yet Chānakya has shown advantages of changing organization which is given elsewhere, employees, ``Employees Behaviour towards Employer'' (P.157).

The Edge of Smaller Places

Chānakya led others through examples. He lived in a very simple way and had great and the most practical thoughts. He preferred smaller places. The smaller places have a clear edge over the metros.

In India smaller markets are cash markets; and smaller places have latent talent. For talent search and for consumption of the produce smaller places are really very suitable. It was the place from where Chānakya got Chandragupta who became a Chakravarti Samrāt; and from such places he collected an army of dedicated persons. Gandhiji laid a lot of stress on it as well as cottage industry in order to foster the people and their talent. Of late, the big organizations have realized this small fact of the potentialities of smaller places; and as a result they have created smallest possible packs of their products that have sold like hot cakes. Naturally, they are sending their marketing officers and appointing area managers. They have appointed representatives cum sale promoters in all the districts.

Low Cost and Low Risk Entrepreneurship

There were very few people who knew India – from its different social, various climates to different food and living habit. In the ancient period Chānakya was one person and in the modern period Gandhi was another known person who knew India well. Others usually look at a part and declare it to be the whole. The tropical climate from 8 degree North to 37 degree North saves it from both too hot and too cold. In between, India lies and enjoys the changes that occur from very hot in Kerala to very cold in Kashmir. This gives India a balanced climate; naturally Indians are balanced people, balanced thinkers and balanced workers: with knowledge and skill of different types. So, it has a great skilled work force. It reduces the cost. The density of population ensures sale. As a result, the entrepreneurship in India is easier with low cost and low risk. Apprenticeship here costs virtually nothing.

The rural population in India still accounts for 70%. If suburban population is added to it, it will be well over 80%. It represents "big growth opportunity" that must be tapped into and clearly some organizations are taking earnest steps towards it.

One thing more, over 55% of Indian people are below the age of 25 years and needs the infrastructure and opportunity to up skill and educate themselves in order to deeply and effectively participate in the overall development of the country, particularly in the natural living condition and economic development. India has the opportunity to grow bigger, greater and stronger.

What distinguished India from Western infrastructure system is the climate and milieu of the country. We are not in a cold region. Unlike the west we are in tropical zone where we neither get extreme heat nor extreme cold. Hence, closed rooms are least needed here while it is imperative in west otherwise they won't cope with the extreme cold and snow fall.

On the contrary, we need a lot of air and open space. The infrastructure is taking its toll both on the mental and physical health of the employees as well as the lion's share from the capital. In every field of industrial entrepreneurship and also in government sector many big industries at thousands of places proved white elephant and burdened the governments with huge loans because the production is less than 20% of the planned and established capacity. No other example will be needed if one turns one's head towards power sector. Not a single unit is producing electricity to its capacity. Many units are sick or dead. It's true from Pataratu to Kanti. It is because of the high investment in infrastructure. All the structures were constructed first including the quarters for employees but there is insignificant production. They incur heavy loss every year which is eventually growing as loan on the heads of the people. It is that sort of bad investment that the free Indians in 1950 are each under the loan of about eight thousand which they don't know.

Low cost entrepreneurship is always a success. There is a tale almost everywhere that each industrial house has grown up from the least investment at the initial stage, only some two generations back.

That is the greatest reason that low cost and low risk entrepreneurship is always successfull while high cost and high risk factories have badly failed. As a result about 85% of the industries started in India are either sick or dead.

The CEOs must think and plan educating people and giving intensive and extensive training for overall gain of the organizations. The initial investment will be easily paid back in multiple ways. It is heartening that many business houses have entered the field of education and training but sadly enough they are attracting the rural population to come to grown and developed urban areas. They are not reaching the people, which would be the best way to tap the talent and energy. If one is looking for raw and right talent, the rural areas are the best place to look for. The organizations in this field are very few and clustered at certain places. There is immense scope in this field. An organization can succeed even if all the facilities are not available there; and even if they are unable to provide all the facilities. The talents are such that can be groomed with "a little".

Creation from Debris

"Move forward in groups as a part of the mass, not together marching as army. Don't fight as if in battle ground. Attack when the enemy is unprepared from five sides with one group in reserve to in-enforce the weakening one."

"At whatever place you are always be in possession of your sense faculty attentive and alert. Listen to all sounds and mark each movement around with undivided attention with open eyes, clear years and perceptive mind. React fast without showing reaction or surprise. Catch opponents by surprise without giving the time to react."

"Be in close vicinity but away from the central places looking at it with vigilant mind. Mark the movements and read the faces of each one coming out or going in. Divert the subtle energy of hurt ego to the hands while hitting, to the legs while escaping but always to the mind."

"Destroy the King but save the people. Demolish the palace but stamp not the crops. Ransack the pubs but not the markets."

Chānakya had given definite and standing orders to his enthusiastic soldiers and re-enforcement civil battalion. It worked and was effective. He had learnt his practical lessons from the initial setbacks that he got from the alert officials and soldiers *when he tried to attack on the centre with a view to win the palace itself but the palace was well guarded.*

After realizing the difficulties and foolishness of the attacks in the beginning, moving in the lines standing at ease after rigorous training Chānakya usually gave the instruction and announced strategy.

Appraisal

Only an alert mind keeps the sense organs alert. The priority must be clear in one's mind as well as what is to b e done and what is not. Alertness will always give a way out from deep, dense, dark woods of worldly affairs.

Effect

One must save the life in all circumstances as the continuity of life is essential for survival of human beings.

In strange style and short time, Chānakya wiped out the Nand dynasty. In the same ways and in an amazing fashion he brought a big and varied country like India under one rule. He applied all the methods that he has dictated in his immortal books: luring some, creating fear in some, entering into treaty with many, fighting battles and defeating the rigid ones but he brought them together and united the whole country that included many foreign lands of the modern world. During his time they were integral parts of Brihattar Bhārat, Greater India.

After winning the Magadha kingdom, he opened his plans one by one to make a strong empire. It is the way to establish an empire or an organization. He followed this path and made the Maurya Empire a great, united and lasting dynasty.

The whole existence depends on work and earning. The sun works and gets feedback of energy as fuel; the planets move and get energy from sun and other planets and stars; the earth moves and works and stores energy in return for changing garbage into minerals, vitamins and jewels and so it sustains. It is true to all living being but there is greater responsibility on man besides work, earning, storing and saving everything because he has consciousness and conscience both. He knows, he can think, co-relate and save or destroy. But his existence depends on working and earning.

In modern context and language, this working and earning comes under Human Resources and Finance. He possesses immense wealth inside. Nature provides a lot for growing more and consuming in moderate fashion. Man or none is allowed to waste anything. Wastage is ruin whether it is of wealth or health or relation or character or morality or humanity.

Organizations are also like that only. Kingdoms are also no exceptions. Orgamizations work and get the wages. If it is a business organization then either it produces something or provides some sort of service. In both the cases, either they get profit or service charges but **every business is reciprocal, and depends on mutual give and take**.

Chānakya knew it well and hence, he laid a lot of stress on ethical deeds, concentrated effort, hard labour and material. In his opinion man and material was important, money was not because money was a by-product of ability, skill, diligence and material. Mines and minerals are important; land and buildings are important. **Ironically enough, the value of land and material and ability always grows but the buying capacity of money always comes down**.

During the last forty years the value of gold has increased hundred times and that of land one thousand times and of labour in the form of salary, has ioncreased 200 times and the value of money has reduced in that very proportion. Why so? Because **money is not a thing, it has no value of its own. It is only a means of exchange**. The value of a material, a product, labour or service is fixed in money and paid in money. Money has that much significance.

That is the reason that Chānakya in his *Kautilya Arthashāstra* declared that all business and industry dealing with minerals should be controlled by the governing body. Its Capital, Labour, Management and Income must be in the hands of the king, the supreme power of the kingdom. He has mentioned: *Sonā; Chāndi; Tāmbā; Sheeshā; Tin; Lohā; Mani; Lavana,* etc.

Kautilya gave other business and industries to public sector as private property to be controlled and managed by individuals or groups. They had complete rights on them. Among them, he has mentioned: *kheti; soota; shilp; go-pālan; ashwa pālan; hasti- pālan; Surā; mānsa; veshyālaya; manoranjan; nritya-sangeet; gāyan-vādan,* etc.

But Kautilya insists that each business and transaction, related to production, distribution and consumption, must be wisely controlled by the government or the body designated for the work with different duties and responsibilities. The control and ownership of all activities is under the governance to enrich the treasure and to avoid deception by the common man or even officials.

For an organization rich treasure is essential. So, Kautilya has given preference to treasure, its safety, the ways to enrich it, the resources of income, the heads of expenditure and also excess and waste expense. He has thought over them in very subtle way and divided them in different catagories for smoorh handling and running.

Kautilya has fixed duties, responsibilities and powers of each one in the administration of Finance. It is true to *Samāhartā:* Chief of all Finance and Storage. He collected all sorts of taxes and entered into his "Sealed Register". He had *Sannidhātā:* Chief of Treasure to assist and many other officials to work under him. The others are:

➤ *Sthānika:* He controlled ¼ of the Janapada.

➤ *Gope:* The authority that controlled the villages.

> *Pradeshthā*: Assistant to Sthānika and Gope.
> *Aksha Patal Adhyaksha*: Accountant General.
> *Koshādhyaksha/ Artha Kārnika*: Chief Accountant.
> *Kārmika*: Assistant to Chef Accountant.
> *Gananikya*: Record Keeper of villages.
> *Sānkhyānaka*: Census Officer; Statistical Officer.
> *Lekhak*: Clerk.
> *Nivi Grāhak*: Assistant.
> *Gopālaka*: Assistant.
> *Apayukta*: Assistant.
> *Nidhānaka*: Assistant.
> *Prati Grāhak*: Assistant.
> *Nibandhak*: Registrar.
> *Dāyak*: Assistant.
> *Maitri Vaiyāvrityak*: Assistant.

Kautilya has divided their works in six divisions called:
> *Karaniya*
> *Siddha*
> *Shesha*
> *Āya*
> *Vyaya*
> *Nivi*

He further divides Karaniya into six other divisions:
> *Sansthān*
> *Prachār*
> *Sharira Avasthān*
> *Ādān*

- *Sarva Samudaya Pinda*
- *Sanjāt*

Siddha too has been divided in six sub categories:
- *Koshārpita*
- *Rājahār*
- *Purvya*
- *Par Samvatsar Anuvriita*
- *Shāshan Mukta*
- *Mukhāgyapta*

Shesha too has six categories:
- *Siddha Prakarna Yoga*
- *Danda Shesha*
- *Balātkrit Pratistabdha*
- *Avashrista*
- *Asār*
- *Alpasār*

Āya, Income has been divided in three main categories and one sub-category:

- *Vartamān*: Daily Income
- *Paryushita*: It includes Balance of Previous Years and Income from enemy countries
- *Anyajāt*: It includes lost or forgotten property or income; income from crimes and criminals; other than taxes; gifts; looted from enemy army; the wealth that has no claimant;
- *Vyaya Pratyāya*: the remaining amount from army expenses, construction expenses, income from price rise, excess income from business competitors, fines from wrong weighing and measurement.

Vyaya, Expenditure has also been divided in four categories:

- *Nitya*: Daily Expense;
- *Nitya Utapādika*: Excess Expense in Daily Expenditure
- *Lābha*: The money spent for fortnightly, monthly and annual income;
- *Lābha Utpādika*: Excess expense on the *Lābha* category.

Nivi is the balance after calculating all the income and expenditures. It is divided in two categories:

- *Prāpta*: Already deposited in the Treasure;
- *Anuvritta*: Expected to be deposited in the treasure soon.

Embezzlement and Misappropriation of Money

Kautilya had thought deeply about embezzlement and misappropriation of collected money by the chiefs and other officials. He must have collected the information in detail through his *Guptachars* regarding the ways the embezzlement was appropriated by different personnel in different area and departments. He has instructed the king or the modern directors:

- To control the money to enrich the treasure;
- To keep vigil on the character of the heads;
- To stop theft of all types;
- To encourage all related production;
- To encourage the sale of the produce of land and water;
- To save life and stock from flood and fire;
- To ensure timely payments in different heads;
- To see that all collections are deposited in the treasure; in modern context, in the bank and definitely in the correct account.

In 2:14:28 entitled "*Samudasya Yukta Apahritsya Pratya-ānayanam*, Kautiulya has listed eight types of embezzlements and misappropriation of treasure: *pratibandhah prayogo vyavahār avastārah parihāpan upabhogah parivartanam upahārah cha iti kosha kshayah;* and also the punishment for each type of embezzlement:

➤ **Pratibandha**: The three types of *pratibandha* are:

    a. to fail to collect money, mostly taxes;

    b. to fail to keep in own hand the collected money and

    c. to fail to deposit it at proper and designated place. Such an official will have to pay back ten times the embezzled money.

➤ **Prayoga**: By trying to multiply the collected money by investing or by giving as loan on interest is called *prayoga*. Such officials should be fined double the embezzled amount.

➤ **Vyavahār**: To indulge in business with the money taken from treasure is called *vyavahār*. The punishment is to give double the amount.

➤ **Avastār**: The official who deliberately delays the collection of money to harass the people and to take more than the due, is called *avastār*. Such official should pay five times the original sum.

➤ **Parihāpan**: Because of inability or mismanagement the official who fails to collect money and increases the expenses is called *parihāpan*. He should be fined four times the original sum.

➤ **Upabhoga**: To use corporate or government money for self or relatives is called *upabhoga*. If he uses jewels then he should be hanged; if he uses general articles then the articles should be seized and its price will be the punishment.

➤ **Parivartan**: To replace costly articles or materials with others is called *parivartan*. The punishment should be equal to loss.

➤ **Apahār:** There are three types of *apahār*:

a. collected money is not entered into the register;

b. showing expense without spending, and

c. to deny to have collected the money. Such officials should be forced to pay twelve times more than the original money.

In the same chapter Kautilya has discussed in detail that the Chief can embezzle or misappropriate money in forty ways.

Resolving Quarrel

Kautilya says: "Quarrels among people can be resolved by winning over the leaders or by removing the cause of the quarrel. People fighting among themselves help the king by their mutual rivalry. Conflicts for power within the royal family, on the other hand, bring about harassment and destruction to the people and double the exertion that is required to end such conflicts. Hence internal strife in the royal family for power is more damaging than quarrels among their subjects. The king must be well versed in knowing others, discerning ability and shrewd in judgement."

Virtues and Vices

Vices are corruptions due to ignorance and indiscipline; an unlearned man does not perceive the injurious consequences of his vices. He summarizes: subject to the qualification that gambling is most dangerous in cases where power is shared. The vice with the most serious consequence is addiction to wine and other such drinks, followed by, lust for women, gambling, and hunting.

Dealing with Problems

Once, Chānakya met an officer of the palace, Mātanga, on a bridge. Although it appeared to be a casual meeting but it was actually arranged. It was almost noon and there was virtually no movement on the bridge. He was neglected and repeatedly ignored by the king. Chānakya was eager to tap all such resources from where he could learn secrets and gain support at the time of actual overthrow. He was determined to split the opposition, to create suspicion and division to weaken the whole set up.

After casual talk and exchange of formal salutations Chānakya said: "Your Matta and Angas are precious to be weighed in jewels."

"Jewels I have accumulated but honour I have none," Mātanga admitted.

"Honour is the best jewel in the garland of a man. My hands are eager to put the garland with that brightest jewel around the neck of the most deserving person." Chānakya was opening up.

"The lowly figure with energy in dust can't be a deserving person." He was too broken to show his ego.

"Revolutionists anoint their foreheads with dust from the Mother Land. Eternal Mother likes it." He was weighing the patriotic impulse.

"Mother will get the head whenever needed." He promised.

"The Mother will safely and lovingly keep that son in her lap." It was a counter promise.

"I will salute the Sunrise." It was another firm promise.
"Such sons never get swayed by Sunsets." The hint was clear. They parted after formal salutations.

Appraisal

Success depends on the spirit behind the work. The effort is far greater and superior in the highly spirited, patriotic and spiritual person than in the lowly persons with only physical pleasure as the aim of life. The hunger will not generate as much energy as the safety in a do or die situation.

Effect

One should not leave a single stone unturned while striving for success because failure shows lack of effort.

Split and Weaken

Kautilya recommended seven strategies in dealing with the neighbouring powers to the highest official, the king and through him to all foreign affairs ministries and others who regularly dealt with unknown and strange people. With the following mantra people of any place can be controlled. One must remember that all of them are not used at one time. If one fails the other can be applied or if one is used towards one set of people then another can be used towards another set. It all depends on the need, urgency and the kind of people one is dealing with. The strategies are:

> ➤ **Sāma**: Appeasement, non-aggression pact

> ➤ **Danda**: Strength, punishment

> ➤ **Dāna**: Gift, bribery

- **Bheda**: Divide, split, separating opposition
- **Māyā**: Illusion, deceit
- **Upekshā**: Ignoring the enemy
- **Indrajāla**: Showing army and spiritual strength

Kautilya's opinion

"For the guard not reporting to the city-superintendent an offence committed during the night whether by the animate or the inanimate, the punishment shall be in conformity with the offence, also in case of negligence."

"The king or the CEO should strive to give training to the prince."

Leaders at the top should completely focus on developing the potential leaders. Who is a leader and how to identify him is a challenge in itself. One will realize that a person successful in one area can be a failure in another area. Or one who is a successful leader in a particular group may be a failure while leading another.

The leader should be serious towards security lapses. This means, how an alert security person should be. He has to report every single offence committed to his superiors. He cannot take any seen or unseen movements for granted. If the security official does not do that even the security personnel shall be punished. A special focus has to be given to corporate security personnels.

Wildlife and Forests

The Mauryas first looked at the forests as a resource. For them, the most important forest product was the elephant. Military might in those times depended not only on horses and men but also on battle-elephants. It resulted in the defeat of Seleucus, Alaxender's governor of Panjab. The Mauryas sought to preserve supplies of elephants since it was more cost- and time-effective to catch, tame and train wild elephants than raise them. The *Arthashāstra* devotes a few chapters to it and unambiguously specifies the responsibilities of officials such as the *Protector of the Elephant Forests.*

On the border of the forest, the king should establish a forest for elephants guarded by foresters. The superintendent will, with the help of the guards, protect the elephants whether along the mountain, along a river, along lakes, or in marshy tracts. They should kill anyone slaying an elephant.

The *Arthashāstra* also reveals that the Mauryas designated specific forests to protect supplies of timber, as well as lions and tigers, for skins. Elsewhere the *Protector of Animals* also worked to eliminate thieves, tigers, and other predators to render the woods safe for grazing cattle.

Present rulers and administrators lack those qualities laid down by Kautilya. It is highly desirable and needed that they are endowed with similar qualities and rise up to similar height. In countries where the forests are, the progress has been meteoric, both macro and micro.

In the 2nd *Adhikaran*, 24th *Prakaran* and 8th *Adhyāya*, Kautilya enlists 40 ways of scams. If the scam is not proved then the complainant should be punished, but if the complaint is proved, then both physical and financial punishments must be given to the related person. No one should be forgiven or allowed to move scot free: *Anishpanne shāriram haiyah anyam wā dandam labhet; na cha anugrāhya.* If the scam is proved 1/6th of the amount, *shatam ansham labhet,* should be given to the informer but if the informer or the complainant accepts bribe and turns in favour of the culprit then he should be sentenced to death:

> *Nishpatau nikshipedvadam ātmānam wāpawahyayet;*
> *Abhiyukta upajāpātu suchako badham āpanuyāt.*

Documentation Skill: Shāsanādhikār

In the 2nd Adhikaran, 2:26:10 Kautilya has talked not only about keeping an eye on the officials and knowing about their moral and immoral character, sincerity or dishonesty, but he has gone to the extent to declare that everything should be in black and white. There must be written treaties and written orders. Not only this, he has discussed types of documents, how to prepare the documents and what type of errors can one commit while preparing a document.

His advice about writing is modern. What a great thinking thousands of years back!

> *Jātim kulam sthān vayah shrutāni karma-*
> *artha- sheel- anyath desha kālau;*
> *Yauna anubandham cha samikshya kārye*
> *lekham vidadhyār purush anurupam.*

One must mention complete introduction and address like name, place, faith, age, ability, work, wealth, moral character, country, marital status, and relation. In the document the following five things must be maintained:

➤ **Arthakram**: Sequence in meaning; main points and sub points;

➤ **Artha sambandha**: Coherence in meaning; without contradiction;

➤ **Paripurnatā**: Everything entered well; using only meaningful and effective words;

➤ **Mādhurya**: Use of known and common words;

➤ **Spastatā**: Clarity in meaning; using simple, apt and appropriate words

Then he discusses different types of writing and even correctness in *vākya*, sentence, how to write, what to write and what not to write. In this context he lists many weaknesses in writing like *akrānyi; vyāghāt; punarukta; apashabda* and *samplava*. He declares that a letter can have any one or more than one of the following as the subject matter:

Ākhyān: suggestions   *Arthanā*: request
Prasansā: admiration   *Prichchhā*: enquiry

Nindā: blame	*Nishedha*: negation
Pratyākhān: denial	*Upālambha*: complain
Pratishedha: order to stop	*Chodanā*: encouraging
Sāntvanā: consolation	*Abhyupapatti*: readiness to help

It is undoubtedly a great book for people in different business and for those who are controlling a business. One example will be sufficient. In 2:27:11, *Kosha-Pravesha-Ratna-Parikshā*, Kautilya has discussed all the varieties and qualities of not only pearl- and diamond- like jewels, but also of wool. It is something wonderful and unbelievable that during those days people considered such things in such painstaking detail. In the next three–four chapters he has discussed gold, its tests, the duties of the chief gold keeper; how to maintain stock of gold and granary; forests; sale management, etc. It shows his knowledge of trees, furniture wood, diseases, etc., in minute detail.

Panyādhyaksha: Sale Management

Internal Sales

In the chapter 2:32:16, *Panyādhyaksha*, Kautilya has given some hints as insight into sales management. Now it is obvious that most of the subtle techniques of sales management were given by Chānakya and are in vogue since his time. There is hardly any change in it.

The very first instruction deals with the produce from water and land. The sale of goods through waterways and land is a part of it. He suggests first to gather information regarding regularly sold commodities and rarely sold commodity; costly articles, *bahumulya*; and cheap articles, *alpa mulya*; that which the consumers like and purchase, which is in constant demand, *mānga*; and that which the consumers don't like, are disinterested in, and rarely purchase, *aruchikar*. It is a very clear indication that one must know the need and mood of the market if one has to succeed in business:

Panya adhyakshah sthal-jalajānām nānā-vidhānā panyānām sthal
atha vāri patha upāyātānām sār-phalgāarghāntaram
priya-apriyatā cha vidyāt.

He should also collect and keep information ready about the right and ripe time to sell a particular commodity and to buy it; the right time to reduce the stock and to fill the godown: *vikshepa sankshep kraya vikraya prayoga kālān.*

The commodity which is available in abundance should be delicately handled, first the price should be raised to create havoc and when the profit has come then to reduce the price to bring the existing stock to normal:

Yachcha panyam prachuram syātād yekikrity ārgham āropayet.
Prāpte arghe vārghāh anantaram kāryet.

If an article is sold at different places then all the traders should sell it at the same price: *bahumukham wā rāja panyam vaidehakāh kritārgham vikri-niran.*

If the price comes down while in sale then it should be covered up by the traders: *Chheda-anurupam cha vaidharanam dadyuh.*

Import and Export

The products of one's own kingdom should be sold at one particular and fixed place. The produce from other countries should be sold at different places: *swa-bhumija-anām rāja-panyānām-yeka-mukham vyavahāram sthāpayet; par-bhumi jānānām-aneka-mukham.*

The sale of national products and imported articles should be so managed that the citizens are not harassed: *ubhayam cha prajā-nāma-anugrahena vikrāpayet.* It should be immediately stopped if the citizens feel harassed: *sthulam api cha lābham prajā-nāma aupaghātikam vārayet.*

On the stock in store the businessman should pay its 16th part in tax; if the articles being sold are weighed then its 20th part, but if it is to be counted then its 11th part as tax.

There should be some relaxation in the tax on the "imported articles". There should not be any tax on the commodities that are brought by boat or ship. The king should manage loans without interest to foreigners for trade but there should be tax on the persons who are collaborating with foreign traders: *anabhiyogah cha ārthih avāgantunāma anyatra sabhya upakāribhyah.*

In foreign trade, the chief must keep in mind the difference in price of various articles in both the countries; and what will be the net profit after deducting sales tax; border tax; police safety tax; forest safety tax; tax for crossing over the river; and personal expenses.

The businessman should initiate and maintain cordial relations with border-security personnel; city chiefs and powerful personalities to avoid obstacles in trade with another country.

If someone falls deep in trouble in an alien country then one should try one's best to save both the life and jewels but if it is not possible then one should save one's life. One should keep on depositing the tax in a foreign land in time to avoid complications and to establish one's trade: *āpadi sāram ātmanam wā mokshayet. Ātmano wā bhumim prāptah sarva deya vishuddham vyavahāret.*

One should not venture in trade with another country if the way is difficult or dangerous and if there is least profit. In 2:37:21 and 38:22 Kautilya has dealt only with different taxes from road tax to goods tax. In this way, with deliberate planning he has discussed the departments from agriculture to forest; and from gold to cotton, the appointments, income, expenditure, rights, duties, etc.

13

Social Security and Reforms

Chānakya, a young and enthusiastic teacher from Takshasheelā had newly arrived at Pātliputra, the then beautiful capital-city of Magadh Empire. He had come out in the evening to see the markets. It was a neat and clean place with beautiful buildings and well-arranged shops.

When he was engrossed in the aesthetic beauty of sculptor and colours, he heard a cry of help. He looked towards the sound. A woman was being forcibly taken away by two strong men against her will. She was physically protesting and crying for help. He wondered that no one came to her rescue. He moved steadily towards them and asked:

"What is wrong with you? You are pulling the lady as if you are a butcher and she is a goat. Has she cheated you or grabbed your belongings?"

"It's none of your business. Go where you are going. Let us do our job," one of them said.

"And your job is to forcibly pull a shaken and crying lady. Are you sure, you have been appointed for that immoral and unsocial job" Chānakya showed the confidence of a teacher.

"Go away. Don't waste your time and don't teach us morality," the same man said again.

"You need teaching and beating both. It is highly immoral and unethical to grab an unwilling lady. Is she related to you? Is she married to you? Has she taken loans from you? Are you an officer of the court?" Chānakya was bent upon knowing the truth.

The man was very angry: "Go away, otherwise you will be killed."

"On the other hand, I say, free the lady or you will be imprisoned." Chānakya showed greater anger.

Actually, the people passing by don't show interest in a lady being forcibly taken away by someone. But this one was different and a novelty for no one opposed such men. Some people stood there watching the scene and listening to unrealistic words like ethics and morality. They had almost forgotten those words.

The man showed his thick and oiled staff and said: "Go away at once or you will be beaten hard."

"You may not have learnt the lessons well but I teach its practical use to young and strong students. Raise the staff and you will find your head broken." Saying so, Chānakya put the book he had in his hand in the anga vastram, and taking it from his soldiers bound it around his waist and was ready for the fight. He placed his right foot forward in a position of attack.

Both the men exchanged glances with each other and suddenly released the woman. They had realized that the empty handed man knows the way and trick to snatch the staff easily, then he can give them good beating.

Immoral men have least physical power and no will-power, no inner strength to stand against an ethical person.

Rampant Venereal Diseases

On one side, anarchy was loose upon the villages in the whole of Magadh. The people were as arrogant and sensuous as their king. They were not ready to abide by the law. Grabbing and capturing the neighbouring land was rampant. Elopement and rape was rampant. Social order was broken.

On the other hand, prevalent sex diseases had taken menacing form and the people were suffering from it on mass scale.

Chānakya had another experience in a residential area of Pātliputra. He saw a man sitting on the stairs of a verandah spraining and twisting his body in pain. The face was distorted. His body movement had attracted him. While moving towards him, Chānakya tried to think of the intensity of the pain and guess the cause. He had his hunches but was not sure. He went straight to the man and asked politely:

"What has happened to you? Why are you twisting in pain? Why don't you take some medicine?" He asked many questions

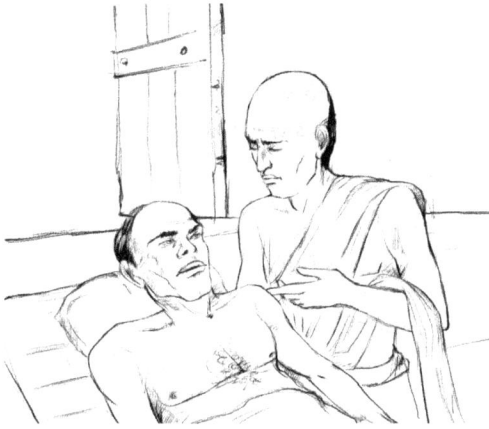

simultaneously. The young man glanced at him and turned his head, then turned his head away but the body showed the pain.

"Don't worry! Tell me. I can help you," he encouraged the young man.

"There is no medicine for it. I am paying the penalty of being heedless. I'm suffering from sujāk, a venereal disease, worse than gonorrhea." The man in intense pain answered looking nowhere in particular thinking of the life wasted.

Chānakya had studied Āyurveda. He knew the cause of the disease. It is uncontrolled physical relation with more than one woman. He immediately prescribed him to boil the leaves of chiraitā, a blood purifier, and to drink the water in which it is boiled.

Chānakya moved ahead but was restless. What is happening here? Why have people no control over themselves or anything else? Why do they indulge in stupid and momentary sensuous pleasure heedless of the consequences?

Appraisal

Control and balance are the keys to success. Nothing can be achieved without control over the self, the situation, the money, matter and man-power. They grow well and lead a happy, healthy and prosperous life who possess control and maintain a balance in almost everything from food to work and sensuous pleasure.

Effect

There is but little space between rise and fall; the steady steps take us up while the shaky and false steps make us fall.

While planning to demolish the Nand Kingdom and in the process of grabbing the palace, Chānakya made many local arrangements and took firm steps for social reforms. When he won then he forced those things with greater vehemence to get rid of the social and personal maladies. He selected wise, sincere and righteous men to solve the problems of limited areas. He started such centres that solved the local problems. His reforms continued. He worked hard for marriages and physical relation with only the spouse. It worked and in a few years the good result encouraged others to get rid of the urge to indulge in sex with many women. Had there not been rampant venereal diseases both men and women have refused to abide by the ethical duties of a spouse after marriage. They had seen the pain and disliked such men. They did not want to be such a patient.

In modern times, people are ready to say goodbye to marriage and make sex free for all. Such days are far away. In the meantime, many have started suffering from different sex diseases including AIDS, the worst among them. It has no cure as the medicine shows no effect on the person suffering from AIDS. It is definitely caused by uncontrolled physical relation with many men or women but to save their face in the society they are telling that it comes from parents; that it is caused by common urinal; that it is infectious. But none can deny that it is invariably caused by sensuous relation with one who is suffering or not clean.

Deeds, Agreements and FIRs

The first two chapters of the third part of the *Kautilya Arthashāstra* deal with different deeds, agreements, FIRs and the judgements.

For the convenience of the citizens particularly the villagers, Chānakya has suggested that there should be three *Dharmastha*, Justice for:

> ➤ **Janapada Sandhi**, at the border line of two villages or countries; at the centre of ten villages;
>
> ➤ **Sangrahana** at the centre of ten villages;
>
> ➤ **Drona mukha** at the centre of 400 villages;
>
> ➤ **Sthāniya** at the centre of 800 villages.

He declared all the agreements null and void which were written and signed secretly; inside a house; during the night; in the forest; by force; by deception or in loneliness. Both the parties who enter into the agreement should be punished heavily and the witnesses half of them. But he has exempted all those that live in the forest or work at night or can't come out of the house. If an agreement has been heard by someone not among the parties or witnesses and if it follows the rules then it should be accepted as legal: *parokshena adhi-karna-grahanam-avaktavya-karā wā tirohitā siddha yeshu.*

He has announced judgements also but the most important thing is that the king has to ensure justice to all concerned: both the complainant and defendant. If the king rules righteously he gets the heavenly pleasure but if the king gives pain to his subject then he is never happy. It is a type of binding over the king also to see that his subject is happy, pleased with him and get justice:

> *Rāgyah swa dharmah swargāya prajā dharmena rakshatu;*
> *Arakshitu wā kshep turyā mithyā dandam yato anyathā.*

Anger and Sensuousness

Both anger and sensuousness are weaknesses and derail one from the path of welfare to the path of ruin. The angry and sensuous fail to realize that they are running fast towards complete ruin till they are not ruined completely. Often, they feel that they can control the fall and rise again but both anger and sensuous or any one of the two don't give the relief to regain the lost footing. The fall continues. Both are definitely and always ruinous. Today is the age of anger and illicit sexual relations: parents and children are being killed out of anger; and minor girls are raped and sold for physical pleasure. In both the addictions, concentration is shifted and priorities are changed. The effort has no direction and slowly everything slips out of control.

Between the two, anger is a greater threat because it can be against any one and can show its ugly face anywhere while sensuousness is comparatively secluded. Anger has ruined more persons and families. Yet sensuousness is not far behind.

Those who have anger are destroyed by self anger or the anger of such persons who were hit hard by his anger. People don't prefer to go near an angry fellow. He is easily alienated. They are usually alone. Because of anger, a person easily becomes the enemy and soft target of many. Anger easily creates disasters. The angry are neither loved nor respected, they are hated and neglected.

The sensuous have least time for important works and meeting and directing the others. They are engrossed in their affairs and pleasure. The sensuous are usually destroyed by reduced income, enhanced expense and different diseases. They are not alienated but they prefer to be in selected company and hence are usually with one or none. They are not allowed in inner circle. They are not loved. They are despised and neglected.

When money is lost only the finance is affected but when the number of enemies goes up high the danger against life also increases. The unioin with suffering is very painful. Both anger and sensuousness ruin so it makes hardly any difference which ruins badly and faster and which ruins slowly and painfully. Indeed, slow ruin ultimately gives greater pain in aggregate.

According to Kautilya there are three types of deterioration and ruin in anger, called *"Kopaja Trivarga"*; "anger triangle" and includes: *Vākya Pārushya*, fiery statements; *Artha Dushana*, financial loss, mitigated and pinching meaning; *Danda Pārushya*, unnecessary and excessive punishment. Since, the words pinch and bite deep and last long so *Vākya Pārushya* is more dangerous than the other two.

Kautilya associates *artha dushan*, financial loss caused to others in anger in four ways:

➤ **Adān:** To stop wages despite the completion of work and duty;

➤ **Ādān:** To seize or snatch wealth by punishing others in anger;

➤ **Vināsha:** To destroy wealth out of anger;

➤ **Artha tyāga:** Failing in protecting the wealth because of anger.

According to Kautilya, there are four types of deteriorations in sensuousness, called *Kāma- janya Chaturvarga*, sensuous quadrangle. After a lot of deliberations over them and after trying to declare the worst addictions, he concludes that each of the four are equally harmful though some bring the ruin faster; some only to wealth but some take away health, wealth, virtues, morality and prestige.

➤ **Mrigayā:** Hunting. It is directly dangerous and takes a lot of time. The time, energy and cost is not compensated by the gain which is only superficial and satisfies only lust and ego.

➤ **Dyuta:** Gambling. It is very dangerous as one out of the two is a definite loser. If one gains then the other loses. Moreover, it is give and take of existing wealth. Nothing anew is procured. What is gained through it is lost through it and in the end, it is only loss.

- ➤ **Stri**: Woman. Both the gamblers and persons sticking to women care least for other important works. It is not their pastime, it is passion. One fights with another for woman or gambling money.
- ➤ **Madirā**: Wine. It affects the very sense, the thinking and thinking process which is always at the root of one's success. The drunkard himself cuts off the root and, as rootless he can't grow, prosper and bloom. There will be no flower or fruit on a rootless plant.

Both anger and sensuousness invite the ruffians and neglect the gentle and wise. Both are full of defects and faults and overpower the addicted person so well that he becomes an emblem of defects and faults. So, both are deadly and ruinous.

Among the angry and sensuous are those persons who have least interest in moral classics and virtuous scriptures. They are ruined who have not studied the classics and scriptures and they are also ruined who have read them but don't follow them. Kautilya advises that one must have patience, serve the old and experienced and control the senses to get rid of the deadly and painful addictions to anger and sensuous pleasure:

> *Tasmāt kopam cha kāmam cha vyasana ārambham ātmavān;*
> *Parityaja unmool haram vriddha sevi jitendriyah.*

Marriage Law, Rights and Heirs

The sixth chapters of his book deal with marriage, rights and share of wife and the heir. He has treated eight types of marriages as legal:

1. **Brāhma Vivāh**: *Kanyā dānam kanyā mangalam kritya brāhmo vivāhah.* When a gentle, humble, wise, ideal, diligent, healthy and impressive groom, who is a good match for the daughter, is selected for her and the marriage is solemnized, it is called **Brāhma vivāh**. The groom's side neither asks for nor gives anything as a precondition to the marriage. The father of the

daughter, however, may give *dāna*, donation; *dahaze*, dowry; *dakshinā*, offerings and *upahār*, gifts.

2. **Daiva Vivāh**: *Antah vedyā amritvije dānād daivah*. When a father chooses and offers his daughter with wealth and ornaments to one of the wise sages, it is called **Daiva vivāh** for it happened by chance and during a *yagya*.

3. **Ārsha Vivāh**: *Gomithunād anād ārshah*. Without any exchange of material things when a marriage and its rituals are performed according to the Scriptures, it is called **Ārsha vivāh**.

4. **Prājāpatya Vivāh**: *Sah-dharma-charyā prājāpatya*. A groom asks for the hand of a marriageable girl in marriage and the father marries them on the condition that they would lead a life of righteousness and follow religious path and live happily together. It is called **Prājāpati vivāh**.

5. **Āsura Vivāh**: *Shulka dānād asurah*. By giving a lot of wealth to the father and family of the groom or to the groom and marrying the daughter to him is called **Āsura vivāh** as it is almost like buying the groom.

6. **Gāndharva Vivāh**: *Mithah samvāyād gāndharvah*. A boy and a girl meet and like each other. They agree to live as a married couple. When they perform marriage at a lonely place or in a lonely temple only by garlanding one another, is known as as **Gāndharva vivāh**.

7. **Rākshasā Vivāh**: *Prasahyād ānād rākshasāh*. To forcibly take away the girl after beating her family members and others and to marry such a girl shaking and weeping out of fear is known as Rākshasā vivāh, the demonic marriage in which there is no human value.

8. **Paishācha Vivāh**: *Supta ādānād paishāchah*. Forcibly making physical relation with a sleeping girl or insane or immature or unconscious girl is called a **Paishāch**

vivāh for the clear reason that such degenerated deeds can be performed only by *pishāch*, the cannibals or the Draculas.

It is wrongly publicised that Hindu woman married or widow has no right of separation or re-marriage. These are wrong notions. Even in the *Manusmriti* there are such provisions on certain conditions. Of course, Kautilya has given more latitude but there are certain conditions that apply.

It is vogue and fashion now to establish business organizations in the name of wives. In that scenario, it is essential to know the rights of women and the ensuing problems about the legal heir. It is essential then to know the traditional facts and current rules. Kautilya has discussed even the state of affairs if a widow remarries. In the case of separation it is up to the husband to see that the wife gets the essential. The financial status of the husband plays an important role. But Kautilya says that if the lady has returned to her parents and is living freely and earning then the husband can't be forced to pay alimony, the allowance for support by one spouse to another.

But if the lady has revolted against the kingdom; has transgressed the moral bindings; become wayward; or got married again, then she has no right for dowry property and alimony:

> *Rāja dvishtā atichārā ābhyām ātma apkramanena cha;*
> *Stri dhana ānit shulkānām swāmyam jāyate striyāh.*

Villages Feed All

For Kautilya, the road to survival and prosperity goes through villages. It is so because all the eatables food products come from the villages. In stark contrast to the emphasis that the *Arthashāstra* assigns to rural development, agriculture, and the textile industry, the status quo in India is that these spheres have been neglected. The demand and lust for infrastructure is so high in the metros and it is spreading fast to villages also that everything essential is being knowingly neglected.

In the sphere of economic administration, India has much to learn from the *Kautilya's Arthashāstra*, and to follw its ancient, strong, durable and tested path. Kautilya recommends severe penalties on the officials of public enterprises which incurred losses, and rewards for those who showed profits. It is being done in the form of transfer, dismissal or incentives. "Profit" was a "must" in Kautilya's scheme of running a country's administration; and that way any organization and administration because all organizations are a form of governance on a small basis, large scale or very large scale or international scale.

Vāstuke Vāstu Vikrayah: Property Dealing

Property dealing is a very profitable business nowadays. Big corporate houses and builders are in the fray and field. The money is losing its value and the properties are becoming costlier day by day, almost out of the reach of the common folk. Chānakya has dealt with the sale, auction, boundary settlements, taxes, relaxation in tax and punishments for deceptions and excesses.

In an auction, after three hammers, with auctioneer's announcement of 1, 2, 3 the auction and price is declared final. People believe that it is a western style but the fact is that it was started either by Chānakaya or his predecessors in India. They had to call thrice and if there was no further response then the auction was accepted as final. The tradition may have been there but it is first found in the *Arthashāstra* 3:65:9: *trih āghoshitam vyāhatam kretā kretum labhet.*

The best thing about Chānakya is that he suggests that if someone has to sell out his land or house then first he should ask the neighbours and the *Mukhiyā*. If they refuse then he can talk to outsiders: *gyāti sāmanta dhanikāh kramena bhumi parigrahān kretum- bhyā-bhaveyuh. Tato anye bāhyā.* But ego and jealousy are playing such a treacherous role that people silently and secretly sell their land and house to outsiders.

The other very important thing Chānakya says about: No tax should be taken if someone invests in a new reservoir or renovates old one or extemds it for five, four or three years respectively: *Tatāk setu bandhānām nav pravartane pāncha varshikah prihārah.*

Yet another important aspect is the way he forces the law and discipline. A powerful person in a village can take water for irrigation out of turn, or stops water for others. He announces punishment for such acts:

> *Setubhyo munchastah toyamvāre shat pano damah;*
> *Vāre wā toyam anyeshām pramādena uprundhatah.*

He moves on to discuss the management of ways, villages, meadows, land management, community works and loan and interest and also mortgage. He has announced different interest rate for different business and different places. He says that generally 1.25% interest should be taken but 5% from the businessmen; 10% from the persons who live in forests or do business there and 20% from the persons who do business through seas:

> *Sapād panā dharmyā māsavriddhih pana shatasya.*
> *Panchapanā vyavahāriki.*
> *Dasha panā kāntāragānām.*
> *Vinshati panā sāmudrānām.*

Wholesale and Retail

In 3:68:12, entitled *Aupanidhikam*, Kautilya has dealt with retail and wholesale and the relationship between the retailer and wholesaler along with many other things like mortgage. He has proposed interest to be paid by the retailers on the credit given by the wholesalers but gives relief if the price comes down before the stock is sold out. He gives relief even for breakage or damage in transportation, etc.

He has devised and explained many ways to test the honesty and punish the dishonest traders, and has preferred all the dealings before witnesses:

Tasmāt sākshim adachchhannam kuryāt samyag vibhāshitam;
Swe pare wā jane kāryam desha kāla agra varnatah.

D s- Karma-Kar-Kalpam: Labour Law

Chānakya is dead against the sale as slave of the Aryans and has announced punishment if anyone including a family members sells a minor, *shudra, vaishya, kshatriya* or *brāhmin*. He has no objection if a *"malechchha"* is sold as a slave but declares that an Aryan can't be enslaved at any rate:

Malechchhānām adoshah prajām vikretum ādhātum wā.
Na tveva āryasya dāsa bhāvah.

The employment must be declared and the wages must be paid as agreed. He has discussed and finalized the fee for professionsl but mostly based on the type of work done by them. The wages or fees are to be fixed according to the work done. He proceeds on to discuss in detail the rules for employment; the salary and the employee-employer relationship.

In *Vikrita Krita Anushayah*, he deals with advance payments and punishments to erring persons or parties. He also deals with the sale and purchase of animals and at the close warns the Judges to be just in credit and debit and also in sale and purschase so that no loss is incurred to any one:

Dātā pratigrihitā cha syātām na upahatau;
Dāne kraye wā anushayam tathā kuryuh sabhāsadah.

It has to be given due importance that all the time, Chānakya is conscious of righteousness and has mentioned time and again that unrighteous deeds will destroy the king or even the kingdom. Here too, he concludes that if religious deeds are forcibly suppressed or if the religious deeds are neglected, then the king is ruined: *Dharmo hya adharmo apahatah shāstāram hantya upekshitah.* It is an advice to all to be righteous, moral and ethical and to do only wholesome and meritorious deeds for the welfare and prosperity of self, family, society and the living beings. We can't survive after neglecting religion and our duties towards Nature and other living beings as our survival depends not on us but on others.

That huminity is behind the thinking of Chānakya that he has written one complete chapter (3:75:18) over rough behaviour towards others and has announced punishment for abusing a lame, a dumb, a deaf, a beggar, a blind or handicapped. No one can make a joke of religion, caste or faith; not even of fooolishness or wisdom; neither of anyone's profession nor of one's place: residence, village, region or country. He has divided the misbehaviour in five categories: towards *Sharira*, physical deformity; against *prakriti*, nature; with *Shruta*, words; of *Vritti*, profession or of *Desha*, place. He was against the abuse towards a living place or religious place:

> *Swadesha grāmayoh purvam madhyam jāti sanghayoh;*
> *Ākrosha āda deva chaityānām uttamam dandam arhati.*

Agreements: Marriage and Heirs

A whole *Adhikaran* deals with agreements, punishments, marriage and wealth for woman; heirs; judgements on in-fights in villages for land, house and crops, etc; loans and interest; mortgage; employees and employers; buying and selling of minors and women; fixing salary and remuneration; advance for sale and purchase; property and ownership. These are all related to well or ill-manged property and affairs. Chānakya had shown the way.

The topics mentioned above are mostly related to the management of movable and immovable property, its disputes and decisions. But loans and interest and budgets are directly related to business and corporate world where maximum of business are running on credits and loans and most of the organizations are paying huge interest every month.

Unlike in Kautilya's state where the king was accessible to his people every day at least for one and a half hours, in India today it takes a long time even to get a "hearing." Some of the ground rules and measures suggested in the *Arthashāstra*, particularly those which pertain to matters relating to budget, accounts and audit, are applicable to present day India. In Kautilya's state, the king could severely punish the corrupt officials, however highly they were placed. In India, those in political office are rarely convicted even if they are corrupt or proved guilty of committing certain offences.

Kautilya clearly states that the management should be such that neither the loaner nor the seeker; neither the seller nor the purchaser is the loser:

> *Dātā pratigrahitā cha shyātām na upahatau yathā;*
> *Dāne kraye wā anushayam tathā kuryuh sabhāsadah.*

The official must work sincerely and without prejudice:

> *Yevam kāryāni dharmasthāh kuryuh achhala- darshinah;*
> *Samāh sarveshu bhāveshu vishwāsyā loka- sampriyāh.*

14

Steady Economy

Chānakya invented and employed many methods to keep the flow of deposits to the treasure and to restrict the withdrawl to the most needed. He did not like wastage of anything: energy, time, money, skill, wisdom, and knowledge, and of course, resources. The resources should never dry out. If dried, it would spell doom.

Chief Executives and their Salary

Kautilya has divided chief executives into three categories, and fixed their salary: 48,000 *panas* per annum to the first category; just half, 24,000 *panas* per annum for the second category, and again the half of it 12,000 *panas* per annum for the third category. The following are the three categories:

First Category

➤ *Mantri*: Minister;

➤ *Purohit*: Chief Executive;

➤ *Senāpati*: Chief of Army;

➤ *Yuvarāja*: Prince;

Second Category

➤ *Dauvārika*: Chief of the palace;

➤ *Antavanshika*: Chief of domestic affairs;

- *Prashāstri* or *Prashāstā*: Chief of Prisons;
- *Samāhartā*: Chief of all stores;
- *Sannidhātā*: Chief of Treasure;

Third Category
- *Pradeshtā*: Chief of Public Relations;
- *Nāyak*: Chief of a section of the Army;
- *Paur*: Chief Administrative Officer of the capital city;
- *Vyāvāhārika*: Chief Justice;
- *Kārmātika*: Chief of Mines;
- *Sabhya*: Chairman of the Council of Ministers;
- *Dandapāl*: Chief Civil Officer of Army;
- *Antapāl* or *Rāshtrāntpāl*: Chief of the Frontiers;
- *Durgapāl*: Chief of Defense

Steady economy has become a dream which was a fact some four decades ago. In the earlier chapter, Kautilya had identified several areas of State intervention to facilitate the economic life of the country. They are as follows:

- The superintendent of slaughterhouse
- The superintendent of prostitutes
- The superintendent of ships
- The superintendent of passports
- The office of the city superintendent

Kautilya's idea of the Passport corresponds to the modern version of this document that facilitates movement of people. This is perhaps the first instance of an institutionalized concept of passports that regulate the flow of people across borders.

Kautilya said that "whoever is provided with a pass shall be at liberty to enter or go out of the country."

Fixation of Salary from Top to Bottom

In 5:91:3, *Bhritya Bharaniyam*, Kautilya has fixed the salary for each of the employees in different cadre and for different work. The salary is given in *Pana*, the money in vogue at that time. But there is a general trend. He has fixed a salary for the highest cadre and the next higher cadre will get half of the salary of first grade; and the next cadre half of the salary of the second grade and so on. It can be understood like this: A=A; B=A/2; C=B/2; D=C/2; E=D/2, and so on.

He put stress on the fostering and security of the employees and their family. It is up to the managing authorities, the officials in particular but the governance and the king in general to ensure the security and safety of body and rights of the citizens or the employees.

In the same way, very heavy punishment should be given to the employees, whosoever, he/she may be if he/she tries to deceive in any way.

Kautilya realized that the role of the State was to ensure that commercial activities do not violate laws or are harmful for the consumer and if the State did not establish and enforce codes of conduct, it would, in fact, raise transaction costs. The lack of trust and guarantee of quality would diminish commerce and increase search and verification costs for agents undertaking commercial transactions.

Anujivi Vritam: Employees Behaviour towards Employer

An employee must lay certain conditions before the employer. Boldly tell your boss before appointment:

- "Such persons should not be asked to assess me or pass comments on my deeds and words who have no intelligence and are not versed in religious and moral teachings."
- "You won't indulge in fight or competetion against a powerful person or against someone who has powerful adviser".
- "I must not be punished at sudden anger or rush of blood".
- "The conditions of my appointments should not be made public".
- "You must honour my advice when I symbolically warn you".
- "These conditions must be fulfilled".
- Kautilya has some sacred suggestions for the employees. The employees must keep them in mind and must follow them.
- One should accept employment only with an *ātma sampanna*, self organized Boss, with or without wise counselors.
- Maintain a reasonable distance from the Boss. Be neither very close nor very far away.
- Never blame the Boss; never behave with him in uncivilized manner; never tell a lie; and never narrate unbelievable incidents.
- Do not speak in loud voice. Don't clear throat or cough while speaking.
- Don't speak to him in the presence of a person of equal status.
- Don't either accept or refuse a scandal.

- Don't behave like the Boss or like a cheat.
- Don't wink in his presence.
- Don't show strain or consternation.
- Don't fall in dispute with his relatives, ladies or near and dear ones of ladies.
- Don't create relationship with his enemies.
- Don't repeat the same thing many times.
- Don't make a group among employees.
- Inform him immediately if something is really very important.
- Neither be a sycophant nor a backbiter.
- Don't pass information regarding colleagues.
- If you need favour, don't tell directly. Pass it on through someone close to your Boss.
- If you need favour for others, say it at the right time in right manner.
- Talk only which is righteous and necessary for prosperity:

  Aheen kālam rājārtham swārtham priya hitaih sah;
  Parārtham desha kāle cha bruyād dharma artha sanghitam.

- With his permission, you can say something favourable, even if it is not sweet.
- Don't say anything unfavourable or bitter truth.

  Prishtah priya hitam bruyānna bruyād hitam priyam;
  Apriyam wā hitam bruyāchchhrinvato anumato mithah.

- When the Boss laughs, laugh pleasantly but never loudly.
- Keep silence if afraid of telling the truth.

- Don't say yourself but send a message regarding disgusting news.

- If some responsibility befalls forgive, and endure its result.

- Be careful. The master can destroy you and your family or can make you prosperous.

Then in the next chapter *Samaya Chārikam*, Kautilya makes it clear how one can know whether the master is pleased or angry. He has given the reasons in minute detail which is important for those that have their work with or around their master.

15

Pragmatic Approach

Throughout his life, Chānakya tried to achieve balance by controlling his anger and emotions but all the time he found himself on this extreme or that extreme. This made him more determined to search out a balancing point in everything that came before him. He tried to see the incidents with a detached view but his ego overruled the balancing factors and guided him to take extreme steps. He too knew that his task was not that of a householder leading a social and family life. How can one think of being balanced when there is war looming large, and conspiracy taking place at many places for different things and with cunning aims? He had to give proper answer which was definitely retaliation in battles and nipping the conspiracies while a bud.

It is one great reason that barring the heads of the organizations, he has taught balanced view and action for all else. Even for the heads of the states or organization he has suggested to collect and keep information and weigh the proofs before taking the final decision.

To the best of his abilities, Chānakya also tried to delay the matters and think in a balanced way. This gave him a wider scope, to gauge both ends, the edges and the centre. As a result, Chānakya was everywhere. He was so effective that no one dared to ignore him. Even in modern context, those who will read, understand and follow him will never get defeated. A very happy and prosperous life is ensured for those who achieve balance in life, i.e. in everything from personal to universal; from family to international; from material to spiritual and from outer to inner.

Chānakya is practical in his aphorisms, dictums and political and economic thoughts. He is the single person who has written almost everything with his own experiences. When he seems to be quoting someone else then it is guaranteed that he has tested that statement. Otherwise, in the whole of the *Arthashāstra* he has given opposite views and refused to budge to the ideas of great Sages like Manu; Brihaspati; Shukra and Nārada, etc.

Chānakya was not headstrong. He accepted everything pragmatic and worth following. He used to move from place to place collecting information and passing orders. In that process, he saw many extraordinary things and had some such experiences.

After raising an army and declaring Chandragupta as the Samrāt, Chānakaya started attacking the Magadha capital and was readily defeated. He was worried. He could not find flaw in his thinking and planning yet the success eluded him. Why? He was worried but one day, an old widow provided him the reason mix the answer. Accordingly he changed his tactics and started getting success. That incident is an eye-opener, hence it is being described below.

A Practical Suggestion

In three different ways and occasions Chānakya attacked Magadh under the leadership of Chandragupta and every time he was defeated. He was desolate. He was unable to pinpoint the mistake. The worried Chānakya was mentally taxed and paying heavy interest.

Customarily, he would loiter during the night to take stock of the situation and to keep an eye over the happenings. One late night, when he was passing through a village, he saw light coming out from a hut. He automatically turned towards it. There were many small holes in the hut and it was easy to see all that was happening inside.

From their talk Chānakya gathered that the hut belonged to a widow. She had a son. She had brought some grain late in the evening. She had laboured hard for hours to change it into flour and then was able to cook the meal.

When the boy started eating he tried to take a morsel from the middle and in the process burnt his fingers. (In another version he took a bite from the middle of bread.) In either case the mother was angry.

"You fool! You're behaving like Chānakya who is attacking at the centre. Food is never eaten from the centre. It's always eaten from a side." The angry old woman taught an important lesson.

Chānakya heard it and was amazed as the practical suggestion was like a boon to him. He thought over it for a long time, realized his mistake and returned satisfied and confident. It's needless to state that from there on he started attacking the kingdom at the boundary. Maharājā Ghanānand was not able to send his army in time and started losing one controlling centre after another. Chandragupta won every such smaller kingdom. There was no dearth of wealth and army. Enriched and encouraged by such small victories Chānakya prepared a practical plan and gave the final blow and won the biggest and richest kingdom of Magadh.

Appraisal

In marketing, it is not wise to attack the stronghold of the established competitor, neither the market that gives him the best business nor its long standing dealers. It is always better to attack and crack to make an opening by taking under control the sporadic markets.

Commodity, Roads and Infrastructure

Kahān aur Kaisā Vyāpār?

Where and which Commodity?

For investment in bridges and canals, it is better to invest near the agricultural land. It is more useful throughout the year.

For further invest, it is better to invest in forests and orchards with fruit trees and flowers. It is more benefial for its every part is useful.

Investment in utility goods is better than costlier and luxurious goods as there are few customers for it.

Invest in the commodity that needs least investmenmt and offers greater gain.

Investment in infrastructure means blocking the money. It loses value and even destroyed after a few decades.

It is better to invest in greater number of animals than in big and powerful animals.

➤ For business, the land route is far better than water route:

➤ As on land path there are many cities for trade;

➤ The land route can't be seized from every direction;

➤ It is available in every season;

➤ It is less dangerous than water route.

> The road leading to north is better for its population and trade centres.

> That path is better in which there are mines.

Kautilya talks of definite understanding on the basis of investment, effort, sale and dividend. Many organization come to an understanding about the zones; some on product; some on particular big customer; some on the quality of product; and many sell the products of other organizations in their area and vice versa.

Kautilya further talks of the ways to be strong and raise resources in the chapter *Heena shakti puranam*:

> To take the advice of elders, learned and experienced;

> To keep the relation cordial with the subject for they give money, soldiers, and arms and enrich the centre. It is like keeping cordial relation with the Distributors and Dealers.

> To get canals and reservoirs for the growth of agricultural production.

To open roads up to the enemy territory;

> To take care of mines;

> To take care of forests;

> To collect and befriend the enemies of the enemy.

By following these ways the weak king can keep on facing the opponents; the growing organization can survive and prosper:

> *Yevam pakshena mantrena dravyena cha balena cha;*
> *Samapannah prati nirgachchhet par avagraham ātmana.*

Collecting and Experiencing News and Views

Chānakya is the first person to analyze, theorize and lay principles for all these and many more activities; and hence, he is accepted globally as the first management guru. He was the first to point out that the success of a person lies in looking well after each activity connected to him, and in the handling of all the men employed and materials used. He knew and has discussed in length in *Kautilya Arthashāstra* that management is goal oriented and a group activity, which depends on work culture and environment and on keeping all the threads connected well and working efficiently.

Of course, this short of industrialization was not established or even invented during or from before his time, but there were industries and variety of things were produced at a large scale and international business among many countries was in vogue.

As Chānakya had to destroy an empire so he had to collect information in detail about the departments and functions; and as the head of a rising empire he had to arrange everything afresh and make the administration tidy and efficient. He succeeded in everything that he did, because:

➤ He knew the art and science of formally organizing groups, creating environment, encouraging people to work harder and getting the things done.

➤ He has the knowledge and ability of subtracting the maximum with minimum effort and investment.

➤ He knew planning, organizing, commanding and controlling, coordinating and achieving both the immediate and long-term gains.

➤ He knew "exactly" what he has in mind, what was he going to do, what were his requirements, from where they could be fulfilled and "exactly" how the goal could be achieved.

16

Taking over Organizations

Before demolishing the Nand dynasty and killing the king, queen and their kiths and kins, Chānakya had only their destruction in mind but once the vow was fulfilled and the said destruction took place, he immediately switched over to consolidating the Maurya dynasty by uniting India. He tried hard in this direction and employed all the ploughs and shot all the arrows that he knew and that looked to be sure shot.

Marriages of Chandragupta for Grabbing Kingdoms

Chānakya thought of the welfare of the nation. India was passing through a critical phase. It was a period of transition. He wanted the security to the country and safety to its people. Greeks were still there. Alexander had returned. He had appointed Seleucus Nicator to govern India. Chānakya was looking out a way to make him friend and grab the kingdom which was still under his control. He knew well about his daughter Helen, also known as Cornelia. He planned the marriage of Chandragupta with Helen.

He announced his decision to his dear pupil and king. Chandragupta was in a fix. He was not in a position to deny his mentor but he secretly loved a girl named Chitrā. He wanted to marry her. He was looking for an opportune moment to declare his intention. Chānkya knew everything. He had planned everything. He had to consolidate the position. Chandragupta got the opportunity and declared his love and willingness to marry Chitrā. Chānakya was not lenient. He did

not listen to the king and forced him to marry Cornelia. The king had to surrender to his Guru.

In all probability the marriage was solemnized in 305 BC, when Seleucus Nicator was defeated in the battle. As dowry and as the defeated general, he gave four big provinces to Chānakya. They were Kabul, Kandhār, Herāt and Makarān. Appius has described the war. Other details are available in Indica written by Megasthenese.

Chānakya did not stop here. He had yet another kingdom in his eyes. The king had only a daughter named Durdha. He was sure to get that kingdom in dowry. He announced marriage to be performed. Again Chandragupta opposed and again Chānakya silenced him saying that lesser things are sacrificed for greater gains. The king surrendered and the marriage was solemnized.

It's also claimed that later on Chandragupta married Chitrā. He informed Chānakya that he has promised Chitrā to marry her and despite two marriages she is hopeful and waiting for him. (This theme has been dramatically and poetically given the form of a play entitled Chandragupta by Jaishankar Prasad, a famous poet and dramatist of Hindi.) By then his mission was almost finished so Chānakya did not oppose that marriage. He got it performed as he had done the others.

Labdha Prashanam: Taking Over an Organization

When one takes over an organization three conditions arise. It may be *nava lābh*, fresh gain; it may be *bhuta purva lābha*, own lost organization; or *pitraya lābha*, it may be own organization lost by father or forefathers. After gaining or regaining, some precautions are to be taken:

➤ **Nava Lābha:** In all the cases, the faith of the employees must be won over. In new gain, the CEO, MD, or Director, must do something extra and righteous to establish that he is far superior to the earlier Chief. The qualities of the ex-Chief should be overwhelmingly replaced by the qualities of the new Chief. He must do some righteous and meritorious deeds; show sympathy and compassion; and put in the mind of the employees that he is a better judge of the situation and a far superior and kind administrator. He should show interest in social, political, religious and organizational meetings and congregations.

➤ **Purva Lābha:** When one regains one's lost organization then he should never repeat the mistakes that he committed earlier. He must get rid of all his faults, defects and ignorance. He must enrich the qualities which helped him regain the organization.

> **Pitraya Lābha:** If some faults in his father caused the loss then it is up to the son who has regained it to hide the faults and mistakes and advertise well the good qualities that the father or forefathers possessed.

In all the three cases, the new Chief must follow the good qualities that were lacking in that organization. He must encourage the religious, righteous, and ethical persons. He should never allow the unrighteous, non-religious and unethical deeds and ideas germinate in that organization. He must stop the entry of non-religious and deceptive persons:

Charitram akritam dharmyam kritam cha anyaih pravartyet;
Pravartyenna cha dharmyam kritam cha anyaih nivartayet.

One thing must be marked and taken into consideration about Chānakya that he seems to be at the extreme end of destruction and at the extreme end of creation and re-establishment as well, but his aim is always to achieve a balance between the two edges, two extremes. He leads the best life who lives a balanced life trying to achieve greatness in all the four pursuits; not in one, two or three.

Theories and Practise

Chānakya used and utilized all the *Nities*: ways and methods, to take over other kingdoms. He used them all: Fear, Illusion, Killing, Divisions, Lust and Battles for grabbing other kingdoms. He kept on doing it till India was not a united whole. The Kingdom spread from this end, North to that end, South.

As a result of his efforts, the Maurya Empire had smooth administration and efficient ruler. The government was hierarchical and centralized with lot of staff to make sure that work was carried on smoothly and efficiently. Taxes were collected regularly, trade and commerce was carried on smoothly, citizens were taken care of and the army was always ready for any sort of external aggression or threat. Every province had its own officials who managed administration at grassroots level. The economy was agrarian and the main economic activity of people was agriculture. Pātliputra, the capital city of Magadh was beautifully decorated and had all facilities that any modern city would have.

In the Mauryan dynasty, art and literature flourished and the rulers built many famous temples and monuments. They followed the rules and concepts laid down great advisor Chānakya, who remained the driving force behind the fame and success of Emperor Chandragupta. For making his ideas available for the posterity chānakya wrote many great books that have been regarded as masterpieces.

Known as the founder of the Mauryan Empire, King Chandragupta Maurya is still considered to be the most authentic and able rulers of India, and Chānakya as the wizard who single handedly demolished a kingdom and acquired power and resources to establish another far greater and stable empire. The following are some of his concepts expressed in the *Arthshāstra* on take over, security, expansion and treaties, etc:

➤ "The welfare of a state depends on an active foreign policy." 6:2:1.

➤ "An enemy's destruction shall be brought about even at the cost of great losses in men, material and wealth." 7.13.33.

➤ "A king weak in power shall endeavor to promote the welfare of his people. For power comes from the countryside, which is the source of all activities.". 7:14:18-19

➤ "One should never submit spinelessly, not sacrifice oneself in fool hardly valour. It is better to adopt such policies as would enable one to survive and live to fight another day." 7.15.13-20,12.1.1-9.

Foreign Policy

> "The king shall develop his state, i.e. augment his resources and power for him to embark on a conquest." What it meant that a prosperous state which looked after its people had high rates of economic growth and then the army is always ready to undertake military conquests.

> "The enemy shall be eliminated."

> "Those who help are friends."

> "Peace is to be preferred to war."

> "The king's behaviour, in victory and defeat, must be just."

> "A small revolt in the rear outweighs a large gain at the front"

> "A prudent course shall always be adopted." One has to be practical, be guarded against spineless submission and foolhardy valour.

> Kautilya opines that peace can be made with enemy, purely as a temporary measure, provided it gives time to the conqueror to build up strength before conquering the enemy.

> "Any activity which harms the progress of the enemy engaged in similar undertakings is also progress."

Setting out on a Campaign

> "After the king has increased his strength he shall set out on a campaign against the enemy, choosing a time when the enemy does not have all his forces mobilized." 7.4.14.

> "He shall set out on a campaign when he finds that the enemy's troubles with one constituent of his state

cannot be compensated by the other constituents, the enemy's subjects have become impoverished, disunited due to oppression by the troops or ill-treatment by their monarch and thus have become susceptible to enticement to desert." 7.4.15.

➤ "Non-intervention, negotiating a peace treaty and making peace by giving a hostage – all mean the same thing, since the aim of all three is to create confidence between the two kings." 7.17.1-2.

➤ "A weak king, attacked by a stronger king whose armies had already started moving against him, shall quickly submit for peace with the offer of himself, his army, treasury and territory." 7.3.22.

➤ "The hostage shall liberate himself by his own efforts or be helped by clandestine agents adopting various disguises." 7.17.33.52.

Choice of Allies

➤ "When there is a choice between two allies, the one amenable to control, though temporary is preferred because he remains an ally as long as he helps. The real characteristic of friendship is help". 7.9.9-12.

➤ "The constant ally giving small help shall be preferred. The temporary friend giving substantial help is likely to withdraw for fear of having to give more or will expect it to be repaid. The constant ally, giving small help continuously, does in fact give great help over a period of time". 7.9.13-17.

➤ "An ally mobilizing quickly, even if he is less mighty, is preferable because he does not allow opportune time for action to pass." (7.9.18-21)

➤ "Troops that are in one place can be brought under control by conciliation or other means." (7.9.22-25).

> "An ally who helps monetarily is preferable because one can always use money but troops only sometimes." (7.9.26-30).

> "An ally who is likely to grow in power after defeating the enemy and thus become uncontrollable shall be embroiled in a conflict with his own neighbour or such actions would be taken as would oblige the ally to remain obedience, in return for the help received". (7.18.).

17

Treaties

In the *Arthashāstra* Chānakya had written all the practical aspects of dealing with other kings or organizations. He held the opinion that any treaty is not eternal. One can enter into a treaty when needed and break away from it when one is strong enough. Treaties must be always for gain this way or that way.

Signing on and breaking away from Treaties

When Chānakya had won a few battles at borders and started the Maurya dynasty, the Kingdom of King Parvat Rāja was at a strategic point. Once, he thought of attacking him but it was not his aim to defeat a small kingdom. He was interested in snatching Magadh from the hands of Ghanānand. He collected information regarding the social, political and economic condition of King Parvat Rāja and then fixed a meeting with him.

He met him along with Chandragupta and the Army Chief Bhadrabhatt. He laid down his position and propositions. Parvat Rāja thought well before coming to a conclusion. He was in between the two. After considering the propositions well Parvat Rāja agreed and a treaty was signed for mutual help and no attack on each other. It was also agreed that the army will move without obstruction through his land.

A few years passed, Maurya dynasty was established. Many small kingdoms either voluntarily became a part of the new Empire or were attacked and won over. The presence of King Parvat Rāja was pinching Chānakya as he was in an important route. He decided to capture it.

Chānakya broke the treaty on the pretext of the higher and difficult demands of Parvat Rāja. He then waited patiently for six months. He knew the weaknesses of the king and laid a net accordingly. The king failed to read the unwritten message of the attack. So, after six months when the Mauryan Army attacked, he was taken aback.

He fought with an unprepared Army against the well trained, versed and prepared Army that outnumbered his army and outwitted in every strategy and at strategic point. Chandragupta won and his the kingdom became a part of the Maurya Empire.

Appraisal

Before planning to take over a business empire one must study the pros and cons and calculate the overall gain. When it seems that the takeover will enhance the overall value and subsequent gain then one should meticulously make preparations, weaken that organization and takeover cheaply. It will be difficult to recover higher price as sale will have to be re-doubled which is not possible immediately.

Effect

The knowledge of the market, consumer's need and usefulness of the products decide the fate of an organization.

Ākramana aur Sandhi: Attack or Treaty

Some claim that there are only two main qualities: *Sandhi wā bigrah;* friendship or enmity; treaty or fight but Kautilya has listed six in the chapter entitled *Shād gunya samudeshah,* the first chapter of part seven, as discussed above.

➤ *Par smāddhiya mānah sandadhita.*

➤ *Abhyuchiya māno vigraniyāt.*

➤ *Na mām paro nā aham param upahantum shakta itya āsit.*

➤ *Guna atishaya yukto yāyāt.*

➤ *Shaktiheenah sanshrayet.*

➤ *Sahāya sādhye kārye dvaidhi bhāvam gachchhet.*

➤ *Sandhi:* Treaty; the friendship between two on certain grounds;

➤ *Samān:* Neutral, neither treaty nor enmity;

➤ *Bigrah:* Separation; to bring harm to another;

➤ *Āsana:* To show utter disregard;

➤ *Yāna:* To attack on another;

➤ *Dvaidhibhāva:* Dual policy; treaty when needed and harm when there is an opportunity.

The central organization or a growing organization can forget reducing the enemy to "not" and concentrate on its own prosperity by following the above mentioned six definite and tested ways:

> *Yevam shadbhih gunaih ywtaih sthitah prakriti mandale;*
> *Paryeshet kshayāt sthānam sthānād vriddhim cha karmasu.*

Treaty for Trade

These qualities have been explained in detail in the subsequent chapters. Then three types of battle are given called: *Prakāsh Yuddha; Kuta Yuddha; Tushni Yuddha.* But the head of an institution has some pious duties towards those that help during rough weather. If one gets equal share then *Sandhi;* if less then *Bigrah;* if more then *vishishta.* One should maintain the relation according to *lābhānsha,* dividend. Without doubt, these things are still in vogue in political, social and business circle. Sometimes, the relation is maintained not on gain or dividend but the value of total sale in a fiscal year.

Kautilya considered trade the third pillar of economic activity and in consonance with this the *Arthashāstra* details every aspect of trade. For instance, apart from promoting trade by improving infrastructure, the state was required to keep trade routes free of harassment by courtiers, state officials, thieves, and frontier guards. Kautilya appears to mistrust traders believing them to be thieves, with a propensity to from cartels to fix prices and make excessive profits as also to deal in stolen property. He prescribed heavy fines for discouraging such offences by traders and with a view to consumer protection. Further, the law on dealings among private merchants included:

➤ Selling on agency basis.

➤ Revocation of contracts between traders.

➤ Traders traveling together and pooling their goods.

➤ Safety of goods in transit

Sandhi: Conditions for Collaborations

The insight and depth of Chānakya or Kautilya can't be measured or fathomed. The example of 7:101-102: 3: chapter on treaty entitles *Samaheena Jyāyasā Guna Abhinivesho Heena Sandhayah Cha*; is enough to feel that. In it he has distinguished one type of treaty with another and name more than a dozen treaties. These can be easily compared to or understood as collaboration or conditions for collaborations and akin to modern day franchise which is more in vogue now. If one is conscious, diligent and wise one can destroy the parent body or take over that organization while obviously collaborating. The ways are the following.

➤ **Amisha Sandhi:** When the weak and defeated king surrenders after taking army and wealth from the victor, it is called *Amisha Sandhi.*

> **Purushāntar Sandhi:** When the Commander and the Prince are given to the victorious, it is called *Purushāntar Sandhi*. It is also called *Ātma Rakshana Sandhi*, Self Protecting Treaty.

> **Adrishta Purusha Sandhi:** When a treaty is entered on the condition that either the army will be sent or the king will go alone then it is called *Adrishta Purusha Sandhi*. It is also called danda *Mukhya Ātma Rakshana* as the king and the higher authorities in army are saved.

> **Danda Upanat Sandhi:** When the powerful organization enters marital relation and controls others through slow poison, etc, it is called *Danda Upanat Sandhi*.

> **Parikraya Sandhi:** When money is paid for the release of arrested ministers, etc, it is called *Parikraya Sandhi*; and if this treaty is entered into on the condition of the payment of money in installments, then it is called **Upagraha Sandhi**, and when the time and place of insrtalments are fixed, then it is called **Pratyaya Sandhi**.

> **Kanyādāna Sandhi:** When the agreed money is paid in time, it is called *Kanyādāna Sandhi*. Since, money is paid in it, so it is also called *Suvarna Sandhi*.

> **Kapāla Sandhi:** When there is the provisions that the money is to be paid immediately then it is called *Kapāla Sandhi* but this *Durabhi Sandhi* has no place in the Classical Treatises. When the horses and elephants are given then they are so poisoned that they die at the new king within a week.

> **Koshopanat Sandhi:** In the treaties mentioned earlier the first instalment is paid and then the other payments are postponed on this or that pretext then it is called *Koshopanat sandhi*.

> **Ādishta Sandhi:** For saving the kingdom and the land when a treaty is entered after giving a part of the land, it is called *Ādishta Sandhi*. After some time, the citizens living in that land are encouraged to declared revolt

against their new boss. In nationalizations, the merged employees created a lot of problem which got pacified only after their retirement or death.

➤ **Uchchhinna Sandhi**: In a treaty, when unfertile and almost uninhabited land is given, then it is called *Uchchhinna Sandhi*. That king waits for some calamity to befall on the victorious king that may give him an opportunity to re-take and re-capture the given land.

➤ **Apakraya Sandhi**: In the treaty in which the produce is given and the land is taken back, is called *Apakraya Sandhi*. When something more is given along with the produce, then it is **Para Dushan Sandhi**.

In these types of treaties land is given, so these are also called *Abaliyasa Sandhi* or *Bhumi Upanat sandhi* or *Desha Upanat Sandhi*.

Among all these treaties, *Danda Upanat*, *Kosha Upanat* and *Desha Upanat* are ordinary treaties and hence, should be used wisely according to the need of time, place and enemy for own advantages.

In 7:111:6, Kautilya discusses *Sandhi* in different way and context. He divides treaties in two:

➤ **Paripanita sandhi**: In Paripanita Sandhi the condition of time, place and action are decided and laid there in.

➤ **Aparipanita Sandhi**: In Aparipanit Sandhi there is no condition of time, place and action. It is done only to become faithful and to know the weaknesses, and also to make the other weaker. When these things are accomplished then to attack and win.

➤ **Prakāsh Yuddha**: Kautilya has divided war, hostility, conflict, monopoly war, marketing tactics, ad-compaign in three divisions. When a war is announced against a country or orgamization, it is called **Prakāsh Yuddha**. In reality and even in corporate world such open battles are rare.

➤ **Kuta Yuddha**: When little strength is shown to be abundance to create fear or small sale is advertised as record sale to lure the competitor for different gains through **Kuta Yuddha** which is fought secretly.

➤ **Tushni Yuddha**: When an enemy or a competitor is destroyed with the help of hired agents, killers, criminals and secret agents then it is called **Tushni Yuddha.**

➤ Again in 7:115:9, Kautilya discusses **Mitra Sandhi** and **Hiranya Sandhi**; and goes on discussing **Sama Sandhi, Visham Sandhi** and **Ati Sandhi** and then treaties related to land.

Mitra Guna: Characteristics of Friends

In 7:115:9, Chānakya has placed friendhip as the topic of discussion, analysis and conclusions. Like treaty, he has depicted friendhip in detail and has presented different facets of friendship including the real and opportunistic friends. According to qualities, Chānakya has divided friends into six groups:

Nityam vashyam lahjutthānam pitri paitāmaham mahat;
Advaidhyam cha iti sampannam mitram shad guunam uchyate.

➤ **Nitya Mitra**: Out of love and long relationship one helps the other then they are *nitya mitra.*

➤ **Vashya Mitra**: There are three types of **Vashya Mitra.** One who helps with physical, financial, mental and social power is **Sarva Bhoga Vashya Mitra**, he may also be called *Sarvato bhogi vashya mitra;* one who helps only with physical and financial power is called **Mahābhoga Vashya Mitra**, he may also be called *Yeketo bhogi vashya mitra;* one who helps with jewels, metals and wood etc is called **Chitra Bhoga Vashya Mitra**, he may also be called *Ubhayato bhogi vashya mitra.*

➤ **Laghu Utthāna Mitra**: The friendship which is for limited period or work is *Laghu Utthāna Mitra.*

➤ **Pitri-Paitāmaha Mitra**: The friendship which has become traditionsl and is coming from many generations is *Pitri Pitāmaha Mitra.*

- **Mahat Mitra**: The friendship that lasts for long is *Mahat Mitra.*

- **Advaidhya Mitra**: He who is the same in suffering and pleasure; and won't alienate in calamity is called *Advaidhya Mitra.*

While discussing friendship Chānakya raises a question, which has not as yet been satisfactorily answered; some scholars and experienced wise men have remained this side and some that side. The question is:

Kshipram alpo lābhah chirān mahāniti wā. What is good a little gain faster or a delayed but great gain?

The *āchāryas* have given the answer: *Kshipram alpo lābhah karya-desha-samvādakah shreyān.* The wise have answered that a little fast gain is better as the quality and quantity of gain can be known easily.

But Kautilya won't agree with them, as it does not last longer. He says: *Chirād vinipāti beeja sadharmā mahān lābhah shreyā.* That great profit is far greater that takes time from seed to fruit and is safe.

He concludes it with the statement that one must consider the pro-cons, quantitative and qualitative, and calculate well the gain and loss then make a friend:

Yevam dristvā dhruve lābhe lābhānshe cha gunodayam;
Swārtham siddhi paro yāyāt sanhitah sāma- vāyikaih.

18

Mantrimandal: Board of Directors

All the *Mantries*, ministers were both like Directors and Executives. The Mantrimandal has taken the shape of the Board of Directors in the modern age.

After starting or establishing an empire or an organization one must discuss seriously all types of works under hand, and take initiatives of any type only after deep and through discussion: *mantra purvāh sarva ārambhayet*; works are to be started only after deliberations and discussions.

The meeting hall should be completely secure and no one should be allowed to enter without the prior permission of the presiding authority or the Chairman: *tasmānna mantra uddesham ana- āyukto na upagachchhet.*

If the head or presiding authoirity has insulted or deceived a person then he should never take the advice of that person or from his side, i.e. his relatives or friends: *na cha teshām pakshaiyah yeshām apakuryāt.*

Chānakya has laid a lot of stress on the secrecy of the decisions taken in the meetings and has quoted Bhārdwāja also on this point. It has to be kept secret till it is not fully implemented and accomplished. He concludes that chapter with that if the king follows his ways of dealing with the leading members then he is able to protect all the secrets and will come to know of the secrets of others. He should keep his secrets inside as a tortoise keeps his organs inside his body:

One person's ideas should not be accepted. Everything should be discussed directly and indirectly:

➤ To know the work that is not known as yet;

➤ To accept or reject the known work;

➤ If in doubt then to discuss and completely erase all the doubts;

➤ Partial discussion of one meeting should be discussed completely in another;

Because of the nature of responsibilities, only wise and experienced persons should be on the board of directors or council of ministers: *buddhi vriddhaih sa ārdham āsit mantram*. He gives an example to close that chapter by saying that as a person who knows no scriptures, cannot perform *yagya*, in the same way, a person who has no knowledge of the Shāstras and no experience, can neither give good advice nor can protect secret:

Yathā hya shrotiyah shrāddham na shtām bhoktum arhati;
Yevam ashruta shāstrārtho na mantram shrotum arhati.

Even *Manusmriti*: 7:30; says that tasks can't be accomplished without able administrative and other staff or with unscrupulous, greedy, unwise, and persons infatuated with sensuousness:

So asahāyena moodhena lubdhena akrit buddhinā;
Na shakyo nyāyato netum saktena vishayeshu cha.

The following things should be discussed:

➤ The way the task is to be started;

➤ Men and money required;

➤ Time and place;

➤ Obstacles and ways to clear the path;

➤ Accomplishment of task;

The ideas of each person should be heard patiently and none should be insulted: *na kashchid avamanyate sarvasya shrinuyān matam.* One must avoid lengthy discussion: *na deergha kālam mantrayet.*

Kautilya has concluded that after general deliberations on a topic, the Chairman should again discuss the issue with more than one person, three or four before coming to a final decision. He should not follow the advices of only one person: *mantribhih tribhih chaturbhih wā sah manyate.*

The scholars differ on the number of ministers or director in the council or board. Kautilya has mentioned that Manu is in the favour of twelve persons; Brihaspati proposes sixteen; Shukrācharya opts for twenty. Kautilya has the opinion that the number should depend on the available skilled, experienced and able persons: *yathā sāmarthyam iti kautilyah.*

Handling Human Resource

Nand dynasty was finished. Maurya dynasty had taken a grand and bright start. Chandragupta Maurya was on the throne. The job of unifying the nation was almost over. Peace and normalcy was returning to the Kingdom. Chānakya wanted to see everything secure. Though he was looking after everything but he was feeling badly the need of a Prime Minister. He was looking for one.

One man from the enemy camp had impressed him as wise, sincere, honest and truthful to the king. He was the famous, rather notorious Amātya Rākshasā, who had earned the nickname of Rākshasā because of his tough stands and very severe punishments. One thing in him that Chānakya appreciated most was the fact that the Amātya did not desert the losing king. He remained true to him and fought for him tooth and nail till the end. He decided to make him the Prime Minister to serve the Mauryan empire.

On the other hand Amātya Rākshasā did not like Chānakya. He hated his guts. He had destroyed a very powerful empire. He was unable to appreciate his direct enemy.

Chānakya met him. He placed some plain cards before him and asked him to be the Prime Minister. Amātya Rākashas blatantly refused.

Intermittently, he kept on persuading him to accept the post and to serve the new empire. He used various means to entice the rigid Amātya who had his prejudices against Chānakya and unable to shake them off.

His secret agents brought some news. Amātya was to attend a function in the residence of a businessman at the most crowded intersection. Chānakya reached there earlier and stopped Amātya Rākshasā. He openly invited him there to become the Prime Minister. He told, "A Prime Minister is not responsible to a king or to a government or to the board of Ministers, he is responsible to the land and the people. The people have a right to see the best person at that high pedestal. You have the ability. People have faith in you. You must accept this challenging job."

Though it seems to be a desperate attempt on the part of Chānakya but it was a calculated step. Amātya Rākshasā was in a fix. He was trapped. After a lot of discussions he accepted the post. It's a rare example when the most important man of the defeated king was made the Prime Minister of the new kingdom.

There is a very famous play entitled "Mudrā Rākashasa" in Samskrit that deals with this central theme.

Appraisal

Getting own men placed in other organization for secret information is as necessary as taking away talented, able, skillful and powerful employees of the competitors for weakening them and strengthening own organization.

Effect

*Even in the age of computers and machines the human resource
has its immense value as machines are to be handled by men.*

Appointment of Executives

The process of appointment and the conditions laid down
for each are enough to provide good directives to present
day human resource departments all over the world both in
government and corporate sectors.

In the present scenario ministers are the legislative heads
but in the time of Chānakya ministers were executive heads,
definitely of bigger institutions like the modern corporate units.
The Mahāmātya was the head of the ministers and chief adviser
to the owner, the king or the *Nagar Seth*.

The appointments and duties should be taken as and treated
like the appointments and duties of the executives and directors.
But the higher the post the appointments were more difficult.
The king may work for years without the Mahāmātya but only
the fittest person was appointed. Announcements were made
and the conditions were declared and the candidates gave the
trial. The king or the appointing person appointed one at that
high post only when he was fully satisfied that the works at
hand and other managements will be smoothly and successfully
accomplished by that person. It was open to all. Even persons
from other kingdoms were free to try and were appointed when
found fit. But the question of faithfulness and sincerity were
given supreme preferences.

Salary was not negotiated it was declared along with the
powers and duties. There was no question of blackmail on one
side and target to be achieved on the other.

Classification of Human Resource

What Kautilya says about the army men is true to employees. Like them the employees also can be divided in various kinds. The classification is done not so much For example:

➤ *Amānit*: Not honoured;

➤ *Nimānita*: Neglected;

➤ *Abhrit*: Unpaid;

➤ *Vyādhita*: Suffering from some disease;

➤ *Navāgat*: Newly appointed;

➤ *Durāyāt*: Belonging to a distant place;

➤ *Prashrānta*: Tired

➤ *Praksheel*: Not skilled;

➤ *Pratihat*: Unsuccessful in life, feeling defeated;

➤ *Hatāgra vega*: Without zeal; one who lacks confidence;

➤ *Anritu prāpta*: Who got no opportunity;

➤ *Āshā Nivedi*: Without hope or faith;

➤ *Parisripta*: Lacks leadership qualities;

➤ *Kalatra grahi*: One who raises finger on others;

➤ *Antah shaiolya*: One who feels and keeps enmity;

➤ *Kupita moola*: Who is angry with the administration;

➤ *Bhinna garbha*: Jealous of colleagues;

➤ *Apasrita*: Harassed by colleagues;

➤ *Atikshipta*: Harassed by insiders and outsiders both;

➤ *Upa nivishta*: Working yet disinterested in the work;

➤ *Samāpta*: Unable to work;

➤ *Upa ruddha*: In problems from one side;

➤ *Pari kshipta*: In problem from many sides;

➤ *Chhinna Dhānya*: One who has no connection with his family;

➤ *Vichhinna purusha vivadha*: Who is unable to foster the family;

➤ *Swa vikshipta*: Working among fully known people;

➤ *Mitra vikshipta*: Working among complete strangers.

20

Money, Wealth and Entrpreneurship

When one is ready to start a new organization or a new project, one must plan it meticulously well, do the leg work, take survey, talk to experts and while doing so one must take the following things into consideration:

> **Shakti**: Ability; skill; know-how; finance; man-power; material; market, etc

> **Place**: Suitability; approach roads; population around; elements required and available;

> **Time**: Suitability of time regarding construction; availability of required things during that season; time for preparation; opening and time of marketing;

> **Problems**: In sight; at present and expected;

> **Expenses**: Inclusives of all expenses; provisions for even unknown expenses;

> **Profit**: Both gross and net;

> **Objections**: From market; dealers; distributors;

> **Future**: The future of project after a decade and also after five decades.

Nowadays, all over the world the people are in a hurry. They forbid others from taking journey without considering the related facts. In his opinion, for smaller works longer journeys can't be under taken. Longer journeys are allowed only when there are substantial and gainful works. One must avoid journey during rain or snow fall. The troubles are then many and works are least accomplished:

Sarvām wā hraswa kālāh syuh yātvyāh kārya lāghavāt;
Dererghāh kārya gurutvā dvā varshāvāshah pratra cha.

Money Begets Money: Artheh Arthāh Prabandhyante

People usually claim that "money begets money" is a western slogan. It is from India, the country of Chārvāka and Chānakya. In the concluding lines of the *Kautilya Arthashāstra*: 9:143:5, there is a shloka that declares that money begets money: **artheh arthāh prabandhyante**; money is managed through money. The meaning is very similar, yet Chānakya is more practical and true in his statement. Actually, money does not come out of money, but more money is earned and managed through money.

Chānakya says: The man who lacks wealth and resources can't accomplish his higher desires despite trying a hundred times. Money is managed by money as the elephants are caught with the help of elephants:

Nā dhanāh prāpnuvantya arthāh narā yatna shataih api;
Artheh arthāh prabadhante gajāh prati gajai eva.

Kshaya, Vyaya Lābha Viparimarsha: Loss, Expense and Profit

The destruction of moveable or immovable property is called loss. The loss of money and other things is called expense. One should start a work when there is no loss and least expense.

One should try to earn such profits which are multifaceted; which can stand the tests of time, place, power, methods, pleasure and pain, victory and defeat; which comes in the present and the flow is to continue in the future also; precious; useful; abundant and extremely good.

Āpatiyān: It generally means objections but in management it means disturbances, to disrupt the working and cause loss and unnecessary heavy expenses. It is caused in four ways through outer agents and inner circle or group in management:

> It can be caused by outer competitors and personal or organization's enemies and supported by aggrieved or lustful employees;

> It can be caused by interested employees and supported by outer forces;

> Caused, ignited and supported by outside elements;

> Caused and supported solely by employees.

Lābha Vighna: Obstacles in Profit

There are many things that work as obstacles and hurdles in the way of earning, income and profit: sensuousness; anger; kindness; shyness; deception; backbiting; ego; compassion; godly fear; moral fear; pride; unrighteousness; neglect; ill-behaviour; doubt; lack of faith; friendly with enemy; seasons and natural causes.

Artha Anartha Sanshaya Yuktāh: Classification into Good and Bad Wealth

According to earning and spending the wealth is classified in many divisions which include even the obstacles, and Kautilya suggests that one should try to clear the obstacles first: *Tasyām purvām purvām-prakriti nām-anartha mokshayitum yatet.* After discussing a few artha and anartha, he has discussed *Artha-Trivarga*, wealth triangle; *Anartha Trivarga*, bad wealth triangle and *Sanshaya Trivarga*, obstacle triangles. If the obstacles are from the relatives like son, brother and other relatives then one should use *sāma* and *danda* to pacify it but if it is from general public then one should use *danda* and *bheda* but if it is from officials then *dāna* and *bheda* should be used to pacify them and clear the obstacles. It is called *Anuloma* if these ways are followed if otherwise then it is called *Prati Loma*, and if mixed ways are followed then it is called *Vyāmishra*.

> **Āpadartha**: The wealth that is lost because of negligence; forced to return after earning it; or causes extrenuous expenses is *Āpadartha Artha*.

> **Sanshaya roopa**: The wealth that is used to create doubt and instigate infight between a competitor and his friend or friemds is *Sanshaya roopa*.

> **Arthānubandha Artha**: The wealth spent to uproot the enemy and create friendly relations with his friends is *Arthānubandha Artha*.

> **Nir-anubandha Artha**: The wealth taken to help a disinterested party is *Nir-anubandha artha*.

> **Artha anubandha anartha**: The wealth spent on helping the competitors of own competitor is *Artha anubandha anartha*, bad or useless wealth.

> **Samantatah Arth Āpata**: When suddenly the income starts coming from all the four directions then it is called *Samantatah artha āpata*.

> **Artha Sanshaya āpata**: If doubts and obstacles are created in the above wealth coming from all the four directions then it is called *Artha sanshaya āpata*.

Income and Profit

According to Kautilya the Income/ Profit can be divided in groups:

> *Ādeya*: That which comes very easily; saved easily and none can snatch it away easily;

> *Pratādeya*: It is just opposite to the first one. Some profits are earned the hard way. The person or organization that depends on such income or profit is easily destroyed.

- *Prasādaka*: The profit that gives pleasure to family, relatives, friends and strangers also.
- *Prakopaka*: The opposite of *Prasādaka* is called prakopaka. It gives pain to all.
- *Hrasvakāla*: The profit that comes with little labour and small investment.
- *Tanukashya*: The profit that one gets after working only a bit, only for show.
- *Alpa vyaya*: The profit that one gets after spending only food and lodging.
- *Mahān*: The higher profit that one gets very fast.
- *Viddha udaya*: The profit that is to come in future is *vriddha udaya*.
- *Kalpa*: The profit in which there is no known problem is called *Kalpa*.
- *Dharmya*: The income that is earned righteously.
- *Puroga*: The gifts that one gets unconditionally.

He goes on discussing the problems that can arise out of income, earning and profit. The connotations of harassment and obstacles to trade may have changed. However, the fact that anti-dumping measures exist or that cartelization has to be coped with or adverse terms of trade have to be accounted for in certain sectors underscore that safeguards are essential even in current times and those responsible for managing these measures should be responsible.

Furthermore, Kautilya was cognizant of the fact that the terms of trade were not just dependent on the economics but also on other various parameters. The traders had to keep in mind the political or strategic advantages in exporting or importing from a particular country. The proliferation of free trade agreements in recent times underscores this point because there is a definite political dimension to trade treaties and agreements.

Scams and Punishment

While discussing Scams and Punishment described in Kautilya *Arthashāstra*; the incident of lamp must be reminded to the readers to refresh their memory and concept what honesty and sincerity was for Chānakya, and how sincerely he saved the royal treasure. It was his righteous approach that all else were afraid of doing anything wrong out of the fear of known and unknown punishment that Chānakya pronounced.

Vaidehaka Rakshanam: Saving the People

All the thirteen chapters of this *Adhikaran* named *Kantakshodhan*, saving the people; deals with different excesses and crimes committed against the mass and adequate punishment for every crime. It is solely dedicated to saving the mass from different types of persons and crimals including the government officials. It shows ways of saving the people from and related punishment towards the culprits. It's not only the duty and responsibility of only the ruler or the administration but it's the duty and responsibility of each individual to save the self, family and society against the following:

> **Professionals** from washer man to mason and from sculptor to goldsmith and from doctors to actors;

> **Traders** and **businessmen** from weight and measurement to rates; from deception to non-ordered articles; hoarding to mixing and from interest to freight;

> **Natural disasters** like fire, flood, contagious diseases, famine, rats, dangerous animals, demons etc.

> **Conspirators**: local or from other places;

> **Immoral** and **disguised** persons;

> **Suspicious characters**;

> **Murderers** and **absconders**;

> **Government officials** and **workers**;

- **Thieves, robbers** and **cheats;**
- **Tāntriks**
- **Rapists** and **immoralists;**

Chānakya is very severe towards rapists with strong punishments. If one rapes a minor girl of his own caste his **hands should be chopped up**; if one rapes a mature girl his **index and middle fingers be cut off** and two hundred panas for the girl; if one rapes a girl whose engagements has already taken place then his **hands should be cut off** and a fine of 400 panas be levied.

The climax is that if the king has wrongfully punished anyone and the amount has already been deposited in the treasure then the people have the right to ask the king to pay the innocent person thirty times greater amount in lieu there of. That amount should be first put in some reservoir then distributed among the brāhmins:

Adanya dandene rāgyo dandah trishad gunoh ambhasi;
Varunāya pradātvyo brāhmanebhyah statah param.

21

Crushing Rebellion

One very important aspect of good governance and success in any field depends on correct and timely gathering and sending messages and orders. It is essential also for success in battles and in crushing rebellion. Chānakya worked out a nice way of signaling and passing on information, messages and orders through light-signaling. Such signaling was in vogue in India. Chānakya improved it.

The height of this lighting system was given perfect shape from the capital city Pātliputra to the north of River Gangā by connecting the palace at Kumbharār with the palace in Vaishali to another at Kesariya; from there to Nandan Garh Lauriā with the last one Chānaki Garh. Whatever message was sent through light from the Royal palace was received at all other centres which were reciprocated from there. The palace at Kubhrār was demolished and the system jeopardized. Yet among the remaining palaces the system worked. It continued till the Moghul period. But somehow, the British did not like it and the signaling was stopped though they experimented from Gola Ghar to other places successfully.

A very important thing that Kautilya says related to shifting of loyalty of an employee towards the competitors: it is the duty of both the immediate boss and supreme to stop shifting of loyalty of any employee, higher and lower, irrespective of rank and salary, towards the competitors. Kautilya has used the words king and enemy:

> *Yevam swa vishaye kritya- unkrityah cha vichakshanah;*
> *Par- upajātpāt sanrakshet pradhānān kshudrakān api.*

Distracters: Problem Mongers

As usual and as in the past the money is earned by many people uncluding the labourers, farmers, professional and employees but basically and truly controlled by the governments and businessmen; earlier by kings and Vaishyas. In Indian concept all those who are in business, are Vaishyas. In modern and European concept the business people are divided in different categories and business world in different worlds from traders to corporate world. Despite the divisions they are all businessmen, the Vaishyas. The meaning of businessman is very flat and clear. Kautilya searches out and declares that in the management of a kingdom so in the management of business and industries, there were (and there are) different distracters. Chānakya divides them in different categories and shows the ways to win them over.

People's Behaviour and luring them

Kautilya has described certain behaviours of people who can be won over in case of need. There are four behaviours that he feels which make a man seducible. They are: anger, fright, greed, and pride. The moot point here is why these four only? Many of "Kautilya's" teachings and policies are influenced by the teachings of "Vedas", which tell us that a human being is made up of mind, body and intellect (brain). Out of these the body acts either at the command of the mind or at the instance of intellect. Intellect is defined as the capacity to control mind and comes from study and reflection. Mind is a collection of our feelings, emotions, thoughts, etc. While intellect rationalizes, mind tells the emotion.

Further, mind exhibits three characteristics: it is insatiable, it wanders even faster than the speed of light, and it gets attached. All these things make one dependent on the world. A person feels stress when his mind rules over his intellect. This is the state of unfulfilled desires. Desires create mental weaknesses, whereas when intellect rules over the mind the desires become aims and ambitions.

There are emotions and trend that have been responsible for the ruin of persons, families, societies, business houses, corporate and kingdoms. One must control them because both fulfilled and unfulfilled desires could lead one to different states and create:

> ➤ **Sex**: The desire of sensuous pleasure is the greatest distracter. It is life and life creating if it is under control and one indulges in sex only with his/ her legally wedded spouse but it ruins if one fails to control it.

➤ **Anger**: Mind experiences anger which is an obstruction to what one desires.

➤ **Greed**: When the craving or the desire becomes very strong it becomes greed. Greedy persons are always despised. This further leads to arrogance which with passage of time, becomes envy.

➤ **Envy**: Envy is created by others' success and happiness. Anyone can be envious of anyone else. Envy gives a sense of failure and insecurity which leads to fear.

➤ **Fear**: The feeling that many things will remain unaccomplished in this life creates fear. There is also the fear of losing what one has already accumulated or what is already in possession.

➤ **Moha**: Moha, attachment, is the other state that Vedas and other Scriptures talk about. It surfaces with too much of attachment with persons, places, things or achievements. But Kautilya lays stress on pride as the fourth seducible element in a man that relates to arrogance. When working one must identify oneself with the work but one should not expect its fruit. One must be detached from the outcome. The duties are to be completed the results are not to be waited for.

These are very common weaknesses. One faces people with these trends: one or many in one. The problem is how to identify these people and how to control them. Kautilya has an answer for this and shows the way.

The Group of Enraged

Anger is exhibited when one's desires are obstructed.

➤ One who is cheated/denied after being promised certain rewards (increment in pay, status, etc).

➤ The one of two or more persons, who is equally competent but is humiliated because the other is assigned a job requiring those competencies that the other one also possesses.

➤ One who is in disfavour because of a favoruite of his superior.

➤ One who is unable to deliver results on account of being challenged to a particular assignment. This will particularly happen in the organizations, which have a focus just on the results and not on the efforts that a person puts.

➤ One who is distressed after being transferred to a far-flung area, or an area of his dislike. Here one possibility is that a person is willing to take on the transfer but is not remunerated properly, and another possibility is that the person is not willing to take on such a transfer but is forced to do so.

➤ One who is on an assignment not by his choice and not of his choice. That is, being put on an assignment without even being motivated for it. It could be something, which is away from the promised career path of an employee; something that definitely adds value to the organization but not to the employee as such (as perceived by the employee); quite true in case of knowledge workers.

➤ One who has not achieved his objective in the organization even after trying hard and giving his best. This could be because of a fault in the culture of that organization. For example, at times we see that even after being trained for a purpose the employee is not able to add enough to his function – the answer could lie with the fact that the employee hasn't learnt much, his fault. But what concerns us here is that even though willingness is there to perform but the culture hinders that performance.

> One who is hindered from doing his duty; maybe because of paucity of time, or because responsibility given is not complemented with required authority.

> One whose remuneration, financial and non-financial is incommensurate with the efforts he puts in. One deserving but deprived of an office he aspires. This could especially happen if there is delayed or no promotion (job enrichment), and/or delayed or no inter-functional or to that extent even intra-functional movement, job enlargement.

> One held back by his peers or superiors in an organization for their own interests.

> One who is reprimanded and/or punished, whether such reprimand/ punishment is justified or not, after serving the organization loyally.

> One prevented from indulging in conduct, not in conformance to the organization's code of Conduct.

> One, the credit of whose work is stolen by others.

To Lure the Enraged

Reinforce perceptions that such people hold about their organization by telling them, how their organization and managers lack the eye of knowledge, commonsense and also the experience to see what one is worth. Also explain to them the "detrimental effects" that such behaviour of their organization and managers can have on the organization. Invite them then to join another organization to realize their potential.

The Group of Frightened

Those who have the fear of losing something:

> One who has thwarted someone, that is, one who has pushed himself up by pulling others down.

- One who has committed a serious mistake; a deliberate act detrimental to the organization.

- One who has become known for a wrong act. This act might be done in a personal capacity and not a professional one.

- One frightened by the punishment meted out to another for a like offence.

- One who has seized someone else's work/credit.

- One who is subdued by authority.

- One who has suddenly amassed a lot of wealth at the expense of the organization.

- One disliked by his superiors.

- One who entertains hostility towards superiors or the organization itself.

To Lure the Frightened

These people already have a sense of insecurity. Reinforce this sentiment by warning them of a possible "harm" that they stand from their organization due to its own (incorrect) apprehension of being harmed from them. Show them a safer haven where they can grow.

The Group of Greedy

State of overwhelming desires.

- One who is impoverished for money/respect/opportunities. Such people want to grow really fast in their organizations.

- One in a calamity. Calamity generated out of one's own recurring actions.

- One indulging in vices. Again, this could be both personal and professional.

➤ One indulging in rash transactions. Rashness of transactions apparently involves a financial loss or expectation of a great gain. Such a fellow will accept challenges rashly - without even thinking whether they are achievable or not, greedy of being noticed.

➤ A person who believes in personal gain by withholding information.

To Lure the Greedy

Reinforce their desire by amplifying the fact that their organization rewards those who are devoid of spirit, intelligence, and eloquence, but not those endowed with qualities of the self, reinforce the "fact" that our organization has a culture of acknowledging and rewarding persons of distinction, join us.

The Group of Proud

Relates to arrogance that follows greed.

➤ One who is filled with self-conceit, self-importance, pride, vanity, snobbery, arrogance;

➤ One desirous of honor.

➤ One resentful of the honor done to a colleague, who is perceived a competitor or rival.

➤ One placed in a low position, but is convinced that he is capable of being at a higher position in the hierarchy.

➤ One fiery in temper.

➤ One given to violence (physical, verbal or non verbal in nature).

➤ One dissatisfied with his emoluments i.e. one who thinks that he is getting much less than what he deserves.

Now that we have identified such people who can be targeted for the purpose of head hunting, following is the manner prescribed by Kautilya to approach them.

To Lure the Proud

These people need to get their ego massaged. Approach them by impressing upon them that their organization is fit for and is of benefit to only people with lower qualities and people of little or no intelligence or conviction or abilities; not for people of their standing. Invite them to join an organization that "knows" how to honor persons of distinction, come to us. Professionals with years of experience can build on the knowledge provided and use it to their good. It however goes without saying that a lot of networking is required to identify such people who display the behaviors described above.

Deal with them and be safe and secure. Allow these emotions to grow or leave such people free then get ruined completely in no time at all. The reasons for the ruins of empires and the rich have been one or two or many of these emotions and trends.

22

Departments and Officers:
Then and Now

Chānakya had thought over division of labour and division of departments; the heads of those departments and divisions from sectional head to executive head but the king was the overall head. He had created *Adhikāri, Adhyaksha, Pada* and *Upa-pada* and also *Padādhikāri* as given below. He has used other words also. In this book, the use of those words have been deliberately avoided to maintain the flow and rhythm of both writing and reading. But these words are important for those who wish to know them and also for those who may like to compare with the words in modern use. So, some of the important words are being given below:

Ankayamit	Stamped letter
Ankeshit Lekhā	Audited account
Anga Rakshaka	Bodyguard
Antaranga Sachiva	Private secretary
Antah Vānijya	Internal trade
Anshadhar	Shareholder
Aksha Patal	The head of income and expenditure
Aksha Patal Adhyaksha	Accountant general
Aksha Shālā	Gold testing centre
Adhikartā or Sanchālaka	Director
Adhikarmi	Overseer

Adhikāri	Officer
Adhikshaka	Superintendent
Adhishthātā	Presiding officer
Agradāya Dhana	Advanced money
Agrasar	Forward
Aticharana	Transgression
Adyā Vadhika	Up-to-date
Adhikartā	Director
Adhikarmi	Overseer
Adhikār Patra	Charter
Adhikāri	Officer
Adhikosha	Bank
Adhigrahana	Acquisition
Anugypti	License
Anudesha	Instructions
Anupuraka	Supplementary
Anurakshak	Escort
Anuvesha Patra	Visa
Antapāl	In-charge of borders
Abhikartā	Agent
Abhiyantā	Engineer
Abhirakshak	Custodian
Abhilekhapāl	Keeper of records
Aparideya	Non-transferable
Apa Lābha	Profiteering
Apratibhāvya	Non-bailable
Apratyādeya	Irrecoverable
Avadhānaka	Caretaker
Abhigyān	Identification
Abhigya Patra	Identity card
Abhinirnaya	Verdict
Abhinyāsa	Layout
Abhibhāvak	Guardian
Abhiyantā	Engineer
Abhiyoktā	Complainant

Abhiyoga	Accusation
Abhivaktā	Pleaser
Abhirakshak	Custodian
Abhilekha	Record
Ābkāri Adhikāri	Excise officer
Abhakti	Disloyalty
Āyakar Adhikāri	Income tax officer
Uccha Adhikāri	High command
Upa Mukhya	Deputy chief
Karanika	Clerk
Karanika Pradhān	Head clerk
Karanika Mukhya	Chief clerk
Kar Nirdhāraka	Assessor
Karna Pāla	Quarter master
Karmakār	Workman
Kārāgārika	Jailor
Kārmika	Statistical officer
Kārya Nāyaka	Charge de Affairs
Kāryabhāri	Incharge
Kārya Vāhaka	Acting
Khanda Nirikshaka	Block inspector
Gana	Organization; Council
Ganaka/ Gānanika	Accountant
Ganikādhyaksha	Prostitute controller
Grihapati	Warden
Grāmanika	Village head
Griha Rakshaka	Home guard
Granthagārika	Librarian
Grām Gāmanika	Chief of a village
Chālaka	Driver
Dandapāla	Commander
Dandādhisha	Magistrate
Duta	Messenger
Dāti	Delivery
Dhāraka	Keeper

Dhātri	Midwife
Dhvajapati	Flag officer
Nagarpāla	City father
Nagar Rakshaka	Civil guard
Nāyaka	Captain
Nidarshan	Direction
Nibandhaka	Registrar
Niyantraka	Controller
Nirikashaka	Inspector
Nivi	Net income
Nibandhaka	Accounts clerk
Naubalādhyaksha	Navy officer
Pattanpati	Harbor master
Parichar	Attendant
Parichālaka	Operator
Paryavekshaka	Supervisor
Paur Mukhya	City magistrate
Prabandhaka	Manager
Prāntapati	Governor
Pritanāpati	Brigadier
Bhāndāgār	Godown
Bhārika	Porter
Bhriti	Wage
Mantranā	Council
Sangha	Federation
Senā pati	Commander-in-Chief
Senā nāyaka	Commander

Conclusion and Niti Shastra

NIRANTAR SAKRIYATÄ: ACTIVE TILL THE END

23

Niti Shāstra: Moral Teachings by Chānakya

What is Niti Shāstra? Niti Shāstra is the science that shows the way of righteous and fuller living. Naturally, it covers the whole life and management is the key to life. Hence, it shows the ways and means of good management: self management; time management; work management; money management; family management; society management and the management of an organization.

Chānakya's Niti Shāstra is best among such books because it provides practical lessons for a better life and paves the way to salvation also. It has been written without any prejudice towards any sect, cast, creed, and sex. Because of its usefulness and piety it is the most popular book after Gitā and equally honoured.

Humbly bowing down before the almighty Lord Sri Vishnu, the Lord of the three worlds, I recite maxims of the science of political ethics (niti) selected from the various shāstras (scriptures).

That man who by the study of these maxims from the satras acquires a knowledge of the most celebrated principles of duty, and understands what ought and what ought not to be followed, and what is good and what is bad, is most excellent.

Therefore with an eye to the public good, I shall speak that which, when understood, will lead to an understanding of things in their proper perspective.

➤ Even a *pandit* comes to grief by giving instruction to a foolish disciple, by maintaining a wicked wife, and by excessive familiarity with the miserable.

➤ A wicked wife, a false friend, a saucy servant, and living in a house with a serpent in it mean nothing but death.

➤ One should save his money against hard times, save his wife at the sacrifice of his riches, but invariably one should save his soul even at the sacrifice of his wife and riches.

➤ Save your wealth against future calamity. Do not say, "What fear has a rich man, of calamity?" When riches begin to forsake one, even the accumulated stock dwindles away.

➤ Do not inhabit a country where you are not respected, cannot earn your livelihood, have no friends, or cannot acquire knowledge.

➤ Do not stay for a single day where there are not these five persons: a wealthy man, a *brahmin* well versed in Vedic lore, a king, a river and a physician.

➤ Wise men should never go into a country where there are no means of earning one's livelihood, where the people have no dread of anybody, have no sense of shame, no intelligence, or a charitable disposition.

➤ Test a servant while in the discharge of his duty, a relative in difficulty, a friend in adversity, and a wife in misfortune.

➤ He is a true friend who does not forsake us in time of need, misfortune, famine, or war, in a king's court, or at the crematorium (*smasāna*).

➤ He who gives up what is non-perishable for something which is perishable loses that which is non-perishable; and doubtlessly loses that which is perishable too.

➤ A wise man should marry a virgin of a respectable family even if she is deformed. He should not marry one of a low-class family, though beautiful. Marriage in a family of equal status is preferable.

➤ Do not put your trust in rivers, men who carry weapons, beasts with claws or horns, and members of a royal family.

➤ Even from poison one extracts nectar, wash and take back gold if it has fallen in filth, receive the highest knowledge from a low-born person; so also a girl possessing virtuous qualities even if she were born in a disreputable family.

➤ Women have hunger two-fold, shyness four-fold, daring six-fold, and lust eight-fold as compared to men.

➤ To have the ability to eat when dishes are ready at hand, to be robust and virile in the company of one's religiously-wedded wife, and to have a mind for giving charity when one is prosperous are the fruits of no ordinary austerities.

➤ He whose son is obedient to him, whose wife's conduct is in accordance with his wishes, and who is content with his riches, has his heaven here on the earth.

➤ They alone are sons who are devoted to their father. He is a father who supports his sons. He is a friend in whom we can confide, and she only is a wife in whose company the husband feels contented and peaceful.

➤ Avoid him who talks sweetly before you but tries to ruin you behind your back, for he is like a pitcher of poison with milk on top.

➤ Do not put your trust in a bad companion nor even trust an ordinary friend, for if he should get angry with you, he may bring all your secrets to light.

➤ Do not reveal what you have thought upon doing, but by wise counsel keep it secret, being determined to carry it into execution.

➤ Foolishness is indeed painful, and so is youth, but more painful by far than either is being obliged in another person's house.

➤ There is no pearl in every mountain, nor a pearl in the head of every elephant; neither are the *sādhus*, saints to be found everywhere, nor sandalwood trees in every forest.

➤ Wise men should always bring up their sons in various moral ways, for children who have knowledge of *niti-shāstra* and are well behaved become a glory to their family.

➤ Those parents who do not educate their sons are their enemies; for as is a crane among swans, so are ignorant sons in a public assembly.

➤ Many a bad habit is developed through over indulgence, and many a good one by chastisement, therefore beat your son as well as your pupil; never indulge them.

➤ Let not a single day pass without your learning a verse, half a verse, or a fourth of it, or even one letter of it; nor without attending to charity, study and other pious activity.

➤ Separation from the wife, disgrace from one's own people, enemy saved in battle, service to a wicked king, poverty, and a mismanaged assembly, these six kinds of evils, if afflicting a person, burn him even without fire.

➤ Trees on a riverbank, a woman in another man's house, and kings without counsellors, go without a doubt to swift destruction.

- A *brahmin's* strength is in his learning, a king's strength is in his army, a *vaishya's* strength is in his wealth, and a *shudra's* strength is in his attitude of service.

- The prostitute has to forsake a man who has no money, the subject a king that cannot defend them, the birds a tree that bears no fruit and the guests a house after they have finished their meals.

- *Brahmins* quit their patrons after receiving alms from them, scholars leave their teachers after receiving education from them, and animals desert a forest that has been burnt down.

- He who befriends a man whose conduct is vicious, whose vision impure, and who is notoriously crooked, is rapidly ruined.

- Friendship between equal people flourishes, service under a king is respectable, it is good to be business-minded in public dealings, and a pretty lady is safe in her own home.

- In this world, whose family does not have even a single blemish? Who is free from sickness and grief? Who is happy forever?

- A man's descent may be discerned by his conduct, his country by his pronunciation of language, his friendship by his warmth and glow, and his capacity to eat by his body.

- Give your daughter in marriage to a good family, engage your son in learning, see that your enemy comes to grief, and engage your friends in *dharma*.

- Of a rascal and a serpent, the serpent is the better of the two, for he strikes only at the time he is destined to kill, while the former at every step.

> Kings gather men of good families around themselves, for they never forsake them either at the beginning, the middle or the end.

> The life span, the type of work, wealth, learning, and the time of one's death are determined while one is in the womb.

> Offsprings, friends, and relatives flee from a devotee of the Lord, yet those who follow him bring merit to their families through their devotion.

> Fish, tortoises, and birds bring up their young by means of sight, attention and touch; so do saintly men afford protect to their associates by the same means.

> As long as your body is healthy and under control and death is distant, try to save your soul; when death is imminent what can you do?

> Learning is like a cow of desire. It, like her, yields in all seasons. Like a mother, it feeds you on your journey. Therefore learning is a hidden treasure.

> A single son endowed with good qualities is far better than a hundred devoid of them. For the moon, though one, dispels the darkness, which the stars, though numerous, cannot.

> A stillborn son is superior to a foolish son endowed with a long life. The first causes grief for but a moment while the latter like a blazing fire consumes his parents in grief for life.

> Residing in a small village devoid of proper living facilities, serving a person born of a low family, unwholesome food, a frowning wife, a foolish son, and a widowed daughter, burn the body without fire.

> What good is a cow that neither gives milk nor conceives? Similarly, what is the value of the birth of a

son if he becomes neither learned nor a pure devotee of the Lord?

➤ When one is consumed by the sorrows of life, three things give him relief: offspring, a wife, and the company of the Lord's devotees.

➤ Kings speak for once, men of learning once, and the daughter is given in marriage once. All these things happen once and only once.

➤ Religious austerities should be practised alone, study by two, and singing by three. A journey should be undertaken by four, agriculture by five, and war by many together.

➤ She is a true wife who is clean (*suci*), an expert, chaste, pleasing to the husband, and truthful.

➤ The house of a childless person is a void, all directions are void to one who has no relatives, the heart of a fool is also void, but to a poverty-stricken man all is void.

➤ Scriptural lessons not put into practise are poison; a meal is poison to him who suffers from indigestion; a social gathering is poison to a poverty-stricken person; and a young wife is poison to an aged man.

➤ That man who is without religion and mercy, should be rejected. A guru without spiritual knowledge should be rejected. Relatives who are without affection should be given up.

➤ Constant travel brings old age upon a man; a horse becomes old by being constantly tied up; lack of sexual contact with her husband brings old age upon a woman; and garments become old through being left in the sun.

➤ Consider again and again the following: the right time, the right friends, the right place, the right means of income, the right ways of spending, and from whom you derive your power.

➤ For the twice born the fire (Agni) is a representative of God. The Supreme Lord resides in the heart of the devotees. Those of average intelligence (*alpa-buddhi* or *kanista-adhikāri*) see God only in the *Shri-murti*, but those of broad vision see the Supreme Lord everywhere.

➤ Agni is the God to be worshipped for the twice born; the *brahmana* for the other castes; the husband for the wife; and the guest who comes for food at the mid-day meal for all.

➤ By means of hearing one understands *dharma*, malignity vanishes, knowledge is acquired, and liberation from material bondage is gained.

➤ Among birds, the crow is vile; among beasts the dog; the ascetic whose sins is abominable, but he who blasphemes others is the worst *chandāla*.

➤ Brass is polished by ashes; copper is cleaned by tamarind; and a river by its flow.

➤ The king, the *brāhmana*, and the ascetic *yogi* who go abroad are respected; but the woman who wanders is utterly ruined.

➤ He who has wealth has friends. He who is wealthy has relatives. The rich one alone is called a man, and the affluent alone are respected as *pandits*.

➤ As is the desire of providence, so functions one's intellect; one's activities are also controlled by providence; and by the will of providence, one is surrounded by helpers.

➤ Time gives maturity, perfects all living beings as well as kills them; it alone is awake when all others are asleep. Time is insurmountable.

➤ Those born blind cannot see; similarly blind are those in the grip of lust. Proud men have no perception of evil; and those bent on acquiring riches see no sin in their actions.

> The spirit-soul goes through its own course of *karma* and he himself suffers the good and bad results thereby accrued. By his own actions he entangles himself in *samsāra*, and by his own efforts he extricates himself.

> The king is obliged to accept the sins of his subjects; the *purohit* (priest) suffers for those of the king; a husband suffers for those of his wife; and the *guru* suffers for those of his pupils.

> A father who is a chronic debtor, an adulterous mother, and an unlearned son are enemies in one's own home.

> Conciliate a covetous man by means of a gift, an obstinate man with folded hands in salutation, a fool by cutting jokes with him, and a learned man by truthful words.

> It is better to be without a kingdom than to rule over a petty one; better to be without a friend than to befriend a rascal; better to be without a disciple than to have a stupid one; and better to be without a wife than to have a bad one.

> How can people be made happy in a petty kingdom? What peace can we expect from a rascal friend? What happiness can we have at home in the company of a bad wife? How can renown be gained by instructing an unworthy disciple?

> Learn one thing from a lion; two from a crane; four from a cock; five from a crow; six from a dog; and three from an ass.

> The one excellent thing that can be learnt from a lion is that whatever a man intends doing should be done by him whole-heartdly and with strenuous effort.

> The wise man should restrain his senses like the crane and accomplish his purpose with due knowledge of his place, time, and ability.

- To wake at the proper time; to take a bold stand and fight; to make a fair division (of property) among relations; and to earn one's own bread by personal exertion are the four excellent things to be learnt from a cock.

- Union in privacy (with one's wife); boldness; storing away useful items; watchfulness; and not easily trusting others; these five things are to be learnt from a crow.

- Contentment with little or nothing to eat although one may have a great appetite; to awaken instantly although one may be in a deep slumber; unflinching devotion to the master; and bravery; these six qualities should be learnt from dog.

- Although an ass is tired, he continues to carry his burden; he is unmindful of cold and heat; and he is always content; these three things should be learnt from the ass.

- He who shall practise these twenty virtues shall become invincible in all his undertakings.

- A wise man should not reveal his loss of wealth, the vexation of his mind, the misconduct of his own wife, base words spoken by others, and disgrace that has befallen him.

- He who gives up shyness in monetary dealings, in acquiring knowledge, in eating, and in business, becomes happy.

- The happiness and peace attained by those satisfied by the nectar of spiritual tranquility is not attained by greedy persons restlessly moving here and there.

- One should feel satisfied with the following three things: his own wife, food given by providence and wealth acquired by honest effort; but one should never feel satisfied with the following three: study, chanting the holy names of the Lord (*japa*) and charity.

- Do not pass between two *brāhmanas*, between a *brāhmana* and his sacrificial fire, between a wife and her husband, a master and his servant, and a plough and an ox.

- Do not let your foot touch fire, the spiritual master or a *brahmana*; it must never touch a cow, a virgin, an old person, or a child.

- Keep one thousand cubits away from an elephant, a hundred from a horse, ten from a horned beast, but keep away from the wicked by leaving the country.

- An elephant is controlled by a goad (*ankusha*), a horse by a slap of the hand, a horned animal with the show of a stick, and a rascal with a sword.

- *Brahmanas* find satisfaction in a good meal, peacocks in the peal of thunder, a *sādhu* in seeing the prosperity of others, and the wicked in the misery of others.

- Conciliate a strong man by submission, a wicked man by opposition, and the one whose power is equal to yours by politeness or force.

- The power of a king lies in his mighty arms; that of a *brahmana* in his spiritual knowledge; and that of a woman in her beauty, youth, and sweet words.

- Do not be very upright in your dealings for you would see by going to the forest that straight trees are cut down while crooked ones are left standing.

- Swans live wherever there is water, and leave the place where water dries up; let not a man act so.

- Accumulated wealth is saved by spending just as incoming fresh water is saved by letting out stagnant water.

- He who has wealth has friends and relations; he alone survives and is respected as a man.

- The following four characteristics of the denizens of heaven may be seen in the residents of this planet earth: charity, sweet words, worship of the Supreme, and satisfying the needs of brāhmanas.

➣ The following qualities of the denizens of hell may characterize men on earth: extreme wrath, harsh speech, enmity with one's relations, the company with the base, and service to men of low extraction.

➣ By going to the den of a lion pearls from the head of an elephant may be obtained; but by visiting the hole of a jackal nothing but the tail of a calf or a bit of the hide of an ass may be found.

➣ The life of an uneducated man is as useless as the tail of a dog, which neither covers its rear end, nor protects it from the bites of insects.

➣ Purity of speech, of the mind, of the senses, and a compassionate heart are needed by one who desires to rise to the divine platform.

➣ As you seek fragrance in a flower, oil in the sesamum seed, fire in wood, ghee (butter) in milk, and jaggery (*guda*) in sugarcane; so seek the spirit that is in the body by means of discrimination.

➣ One destitute of wealth is not destitute, he is indeed rich (if he is learned); but the man devoid of learning is destitute in every way.

➣ We should carefully scrutinize that place upon which we step (having it ascertained to be free from filth and living creatures like insects, etc.); we should drink water, which has been filtered (through a clean cloth); we should speak only those words, which have the sanction of the *shōstras*; and do that act which we have carefully considered.

➣ He who desires sense gratification must give up all thoughts of acquiring knowledge; and he who seeks knowledge must not hope for sense gratification. How can he who seeks sense gratification acquire knowledge, and he who possesses knowledge enjoy mundane sense pleasure?

➤ What is it that escapes the observation of poets? What is that act that women are incapable of doing? What will drunken people not pirate? What will a crow not eat?

➤ Fate makes a beggar a king and a king a beggar. It makes a rich man poor and a poor man rich.

➤ The beggar is a miser's enemy; the wise counsellor is the fool's enemy; her husband is an adulterous wife's enemy; and the moon is the enemy of the thief.

➤ Those who are destitute of learning, penance, knowledge, good disposition, virtue and benevolence are brutes wandering the earth in the form of men. They are burdensome to the earth.

➤ Those who are empty-minded cannot be benefited by instruction. Bamboo does not acquire the quality of sandalwood by being associated with the Malaya Mountain.

➤ What good can the scriptures do to a man who has no sense of his own? Of what use is as mirror to a blind man?

➤ Nothing can reform a bad man, just as the posteriors cannot become a superior part of the body though washed one hundred times.

➤ By offending a kinsman, life is lost; by offending others, wealth is lost; by offending the king, everything is lost; and by offending a brāhmin, one's whole family is ruined.

➤ It is better to live under a tree in a jungle inhabited by tigers and elephants, to maintain oneself in such a place with ripe fruits and spring water, to lie down on grass and to wear the ragged barks of trees than to live amongst one's relations when reduced to poverty.

- The *brāhmin* is like a tree; his prayers are the roots, his chanting of the *Vedas* are the branches, and his religious acts are the leaves. Constant effort should be made to preserve his roots for if the roots are destroyed there can be no branches or leaves.

- My mother is Kamala Devi (Lakshmi), my father is Lord Janārdana, my kinsmen are Vishnu *bhaktas* (*Vaishnavas*), devotees to Lord Vishnu and my homeland is all the three worlds.

- During the night many kinds of birds perch on a tree but in the morning they fly in all the directions. Why should we lament for that? Similarly, we should not grieve when we must inevitably part company from our dear ones.

- Poverty, disease, sorrow, imprisonment, and other evils are the fruits borne by the tree of one's own sins.

- Wealth, a friend, a wife, and a kingdom may be regained; but this body when lost may never be acquired again.

- The enemy can be overcome by the union of large numbers, just as grass through its collectiveness wards off erosion caused by heavy rainfall.

- Oil on water, a secret communicated to a base man, a gift given to a worthy receiver, and scriptural instruction given to an intelligent man spread out by virtue of their nature.

- If men should always retain the state of mind they experience when hearing religious instruction, when present at a crematorium ground, and when in sickness, then who could not attain liberation.

- If a man should feel before, as he feels after repentance, then who would not attain perfection?

- We should not feel pride in our charity, austerity, valour, scriptural knowledge, modesty, and morality, for the world is full of the rarest gems.

➤ He who lives in our mind is near though he may actually be far away; but he who is not in our heart is far though he may really be nearby.

➤ We should always speak what would please the man of whom we expect a favour, like the hunter who sings sweetly when he desires to shoot a deer.

➤ It is ruinous to be familiar with the king, fire, the religious preceptor, and a woman. To be altogether indifferent to them is to be deprived of the opportunity to get benefited. Hence, our association with them must be from a safe distance.

➤ We should always deal cautiously with fire, water, women, foolish people, serpents, and members of a royal family; for they may, when the occasion presents itself, at once bring about our death.

➤ He should be considered to be living who is virtuous and pious, but the life of a man who is destitute of religion and virtues is void of any blessing.

➤ If you wish to gain control of the world by the performance of a single deed, then keep the following fifteen, which are prone to wander here and there, from getting the upper hand of you: the five sense objects (objects of sight, sound, smell, taste, and touch); the five sense organs (ears, eyes, nose, tongue and skin) and organs of activity (hands, legs, mouth, genitals and anus).

➤ He is a *pandit*, man of knowledge, who speaks what is suitable to the occasion, who renders loving service according to his ability, and who knows the limits of his anger.

➤ One single object, a woman, appears in three different ways. It appears as a corpse to the man who practises austerity, to the sensual it appears as an attractive sensuous body, and to the dogs as a lump of flesh.

➤ A wise man should not divulge the formula of a medicine which he has well prepared; an act of charity which he has performed; domestic conflicts; private affairs with his wife; poorly prepared food he may have been offered; or slang he may have heard.

➤ The cuckoos remain silent for a long time, for several seasons, until they are able to sing sweetly in the spring, so as to give joy to all.

➤ We should secure and keep the following: the blessings of meritorious deeds, wealth, grain, the words of the spiritual master, and rare medicines. Otherwise life becomes impossible.

➤ Avoid the companionship of malicious people and live in the company of old saints and sages.

➤ The fool, *mudha*, who fancies that a charming young lady loves him, becomes her slave and he dances like a *shakuntal* bird tied to a string.

➤ Who is there who, having become rich, has not become proud? What licentious man has put an end to his calamities? What man in this world has not been overcome by a woman? Who is always loved by the king? Who is there who has not been overcome by the ravages of time? What beggar has attained glory? Who has become happy by contracting the vices of the wicked?

➤ A man attains greatness by his merits, not simply by occupying an exalted seat. Can we call a crow an eagle, *garuda*, simply because he sits on the top of a tall building?

➤ The man who is praised by others as great is regarded as worthy though he may be really void of all merit. But the man who sings his own praises lowers himself in the estimation of others though he should be *Indra*, the possessor of all excellences.

➤ If good qualities should characterize a man of discrimination, the brilliance of his qualities will be recognized just as a gem, which is essentially bright, really shines when fixed in an ornament of gold.

➤ Even one who, by his qualities, appears to be all knowing suffers without patronage; the gem, though precious, requires a gold setting.

➤ I do not deserve that wealth which is to be attained by enduring much suffering, or by transgressing the rules of virtue, or by flattering an enemy.

➤ Those who were not satiated with the enjoyment of wealth, food and women have all passed away; there are others now passing away who have likewise remained un-satiated; and in the future still others will pass away feeling unsatiated.

➤ All charities and sacrifices, performed for fruitful gain, bring only temporary results, but gifts made to deserving persons and protection offered to all creatures, shall never perish.

➤ A blade of grass is light, cotton is lighter, and the beggar is infinitely lighter still. Why then does not the wind carry him away? Because it fears that he may ask alms of him.

➤ It is better to die than to preserve this life by incurring disgrace. The loss of life causes but a moment's grief, but disgrace brings grief every day of one's life.

➤ All the creatures are pleased by loving words; and therefore, we should address words that are pleasing to all, for there is no lack of sweet words.

➤ There are two nectarine fruits hanging from the tree of this world: one is the hearing of sweet words and the other, the society of saintly men.

➤ The good habits of charity, learning and austerity practised during many past lives continue to be cultivated in this birth by virtue of yoga of this present life to the previous ones.

➤ One whose knowledge is confined to books and whose wealth is in the possession of others are of no use to him. He can use neither his knowledge nor wealth when the need for them arises.

➤ The scholar who has acquired knowledge by studying innumerable books without the blessings of a bonafide spiritual master does not shine in an assembly of truly learned men just as an illegitimate child is not honoured in society.

➤ We should repay the favours of others by acts of kindness; so should we return evil for evil in which there is no sin, for it is necessary to pay a wicked man in his own coin.

➤ That thing which is distant, that thing which appears impossible, and that which is far beyond our reach, can be easily attained through *tapasyā*, religious austerity and penance, for nothing can surpass austerity.

➤ What vice could be worse than covetousness? What is more sinful than slander? For one who is truthful, what need is there for austerity? For one who has a clean heart, what is the need for pilgrimage? If one has a good disposition, what other virtue is needed? If a man has fame, what is the value of other ornamentation? What need is there for wealth for the man of practical knowledge? And if a man is dishonoured, what could there be worse than death?

➤ Though the sea, which is the reservoir of all jewels, is the father of the conch shell, and the Goddess of fortune Lakshmi is conch's sister, still the conch must go from door to door for alms in the hands of a beggar. It is true therefore, that one gains nothing without having given in the past.

➤ When a man has no strength left in him he becomes a *sādhu*, one without wealth acts like a *brahmachāri*, a sick man behaves like a devotee of the Lord, and when a woman grows old she becomes devoted to her husband.

➤ There is poison in the fang of the serpent, in the mouth of the fly, and in the sting of a scorpion; but the wicked man is saturated with it.

➤ The hand is not so well adorned by ornaments as by charitable offerings; one does not become clean by smearing sandalwood paste upon the body as by taking a bath; one does not become satisfied by dinner as by having respect shown to him; and salvation is not attained by self-adornment as by cultivation of spiritual knowledge.

➤ The eating of *tundi* fruit deprives a man of his sense, while the *vacha* root administered revives his reasoning immediately.

➤ He who nurtures benevolence for all creatures within his heart overcomes all difficulties and will be the recipient of all types of riches at every step.

➤ What is there to be enjoyed in the world of *Indra* for one whose wife is loving and virtuous, who possesses wealth, who has a well-behaved son endowed with good qualities, and who has grandchildren born of his children?

➤ Men have eating, sleeping, fearing, and mating in common with the lower animals. That in which men excel the beasts is discretionary knowledge; hence, indiscreet men who are without knowledge should be regarded as beasts.

➤ If the bees that seek the liquid oozing from the head of a lust-intoxicated elephant are driven away by the flapping of his ears, then the elephant has lost only the ornament of his head. The bees are quite happy in the lotus-filled lake.

- A king, a prostitute, Yamarāja, fire, a thief, a young boy, and a beggar cannot understand the suffering of others. The eighth of this category is the tax collector.

- O lady, why are you gazing downward? Has something of yours fallen on the ground?"

She replied, "O fool, can you not understand the pearl of my youth has slipped away?"

O *Ketki* flower! Serpents live in your midst, you bear no edible fruits, your leaves are covered with thorns, you are crooked in growth, you thrive in mud, and you are not easily accessible, still for your exceptional fragrance you are as dear as kinsmen to others. A single excellence overcomes a multitude of blemishes.

Asado mā sadgamaya!
Tamaso mā jyotirgamaya!
Mrityormā amritam gamaya!
Aum Shāntih! Shāntih! Shāntih!

O God! Lead us from unreal to real, from untruth to truth.
O God! Lead us from darkness to light.
O God! Lead us from death to immortality.
O God! Let there be peace, peace and peace.

24

Accomplishments and Attainment

Chānakya was not only a wise person of incomparable dedication; indomitable determination and unshakable concentration but also dedicated religious soul who believed in and followed the most righteous philosophy of plain living and high thinking. As a result, he was very healthy and strong though, lean and thin. It helped him a lot particularly it kept him active till the end. It was not only about writing the books and giving solid expression to acquired knowledge and experience but also of remaining vigilant over the entire empire and the emperor that he created. So, even after the departure of Chandragupta Maurya and even after taking voluntary retirement he did not break his relation with the administration. He kept watch through his strong espionage system. Before taking retirement, he succeeded in forcing his strongest enemy Mudrā Rākshasā to surrender. But he honoured him by giving his own post of Mahāmatya and with that his powers, command knowledge and acumen.

Enemy Made Successor

Chānakya was anxiously waiting for the message: What Mudrā Rākshasā was thinking and planning to do. His Guptachars had tightened the net around his neck. He had no way to escape. An escape from his grip was impossible.

His most reliable disciple and the head of his Guptachar Vibhāga, Purushdatt came to him. Chānakya saw him and all but ran to him to know the details:

"What? What is he doing?" He asked without mentioning the name.

"Within an hour he will commit suicide?" Purushdatt gave a confident reply.

"No, it cannot be. It should not be. It will be my worst defeat. He is a greater Amātya than me. He is the priceless jewel. I can't lose him. Did you send my words to him to see me?"

"In reply to your courteous invitation, he said loudly: He can kill me. I will kill myself but won't meet the most cruel and cunning beggar." Purushdatt had his words to repeat.

"It's not the question of my condition, character or perception. It is the question of the safety of the king, kingdom and the people. His life is more important than my life." Chānakya shouted patiently and thoughtfully.

"Then, why did you force him to commit suicide?" Purushdatt had a very pertinent question.

"It is not the time to discuss it. It is the time to save him. The time is passing out." Chānakya impatiently murmured but did not move. He saw another Guptachar coming towards him: "Sukesh! What have you to say?"

"I did not realize at first but he is coming alone towards you; empty handed and tranquil." The Guptachar informed.

"Great! Excellent! Hurrah!" Chānakya was jubilant.

"Here he is." The Guptachar whispered.

"Both of you welcome him." Chānakya ordered.

"What?" The surprise was there but they went forward and welcomed defeated Amātya Rākshasā.

"*Chānakya humbly salutes and welcomes Mahāmātya Mudrā Rākshasā!*" *Chānakya bowed with folded hands and placed a garland in his neck.*

"*It pinches like salt on burn-injuries.*" *Rākshasā could hardly reciprocate the salutation.*

"*You are great Mahāmātya Rākshasā! You are now not the defeated person but the Chief Amātya of Chandraguta Maurya and the Maurya dynasty! I welcome thee!*" *Chānakya was courteous.*

"*It is another joke that bites deeply.*"

"*Not at all! Not at all! You have just replaced me. You have won!*" *Chānakya tried to continue the riddle.*

"*None can win till Chānakya is there.*" *He tried to hide neither his anger nor surprise.*

"*Chānakya is nowhere. He has just taken retirement and handing over the charge to new Mahāmātya Shri Mudrā Rākshasā with pleasure. You are free to run the administration on your pattern in absence of your enemy Chānakya. I know, you love your country; your people and have always been sincere to your king. It is the reward for that great service.*" *Chānakya clarified.*

"*I don't believe!*" *He showed his doubt.*

"*That is immaterial. Take the charge and start working that is important. The first thing that you have to do now is to confirm your acceptance to Mahārāja Chandragupta Maurya. Come with me.*" *Chānakya invited him.*

Appraisal

It is known to all that modern directors are reluctant in vacating their seat and handing over the charge to another, able and performing person. Some fight tooth and nail to remain on the chair despite the record of loss during the last few years. They hope to regain the loss but since they are exhausted figures so they must make way for others.

Effect

One must be free from the lust, particularly the lust of power, and one must sacrifice personal gain for the organization.

The above incident is a free version of the events described in the Samskrit drama "Mudrā Rākshasā" by Vishākhadatt. It shows ample light on the opposition between the two and how Chānakya forced him to accept the post to ensure the safety of the king, kingdom and people. It is a rare example of offering the highest post to an enemy to buy his unconditional support and loyalty.

It is the most wonderful part of the episode from the life of Chānakya that he forcibly gave his own post to his dangerous opponent Mudrā Rākshasā, the Prime Minister of the *Nand* dynasty that Chānakya uprooted to establish the *Maurya* Empire. Mudrā Rākshasā was not willing to accept the post as he felt the defeat deeply and thought himself unfit to run such a vast empire when his method and administration had ruined one big empire. But it was the uncanny ability of Chānakya that recognized the ability of the defeated Minister, as he knew that Mudrā Rākshasā *was not defeated*, Chānakya *had won*. Chānakya had manipulated everything extremely well and outwitted everyone including Mudrā Rākshasā.

With the help of Purushdatt, his disciple and head of his espionage system, he did it in such a way that Mudrā Rākshasā had only two options left: one was to commit suicide, and the other was to surrender to Chānakya by accepting the offer, which was the greatest offer that he could have dreamt of. He became the Prime Minister of Chandragupta, the ruler of Maurya dynasty.

The first was the aim of the second which was a fresh beginning for Mudrā Rākshasā. His wisdom, confidence and will power assured him of his success. So, he awoke and arose and took the command in own hands. It was the greatest compensation for genuine person though defeated. He was sure that neither Chānakya would force nor he will follow his dictates. Thus he ascended and got the honour that he rightfully deserved. The bright career was now brighter enough to damp the defeat in deeper shadows.

It establishes the effectiveness of Chānakya's ways and ability but Mudrā Rākshasā abilities wouldn't be denied or ignored. What greatness! The enemy is given the highest post. It shows man management, recognition of ability and posting the best available on key post despite enmity and prejudices. There is no other example in the whole of human history. Of course, there is none to come even closer to Chānakya, particularly as a person that demolished one running and flourishing organization; on the ruins immediately established another one; reconstructed everything in a very short span of time and made it strong enough to last for around 2,000 years before getting divided in smaller units. It was the need of the time for betterment and security of the kingdom that he had raised out of nothing and from nowhere.

Relinquishing the post at the prime minister of such a vast kingdom, is one wonder that the modern world can hardly imagine and digest; and the modern man can hardly wish to repeat; and giving that post to that honest, able and powerful enemy who was trying his level and powerful best to kill him, and who was brutally defeated, may have low morale and depressed is another wonder.

Phenomenal Figure

These unparalleled personal feats make Chānakya a phenomenal figure. Besides others these two are also important reasons that Chānakya has neither died nor faded away; neither has been weakened nor grown old and outdated despite the fact that around 2,500 years have already passed. *His immortality establishes the fact that he was not of a time but all times, not of an age but all ages, that his ways and methods are perfect to such an extent that all those can succeed that follow him diligently and without diverting from the aim and the path.* His aphorisms are immortal and eternal. Like him the followers got the power to endure and sustain the crudest tests of time, and coming out with flying colours. *Chānakya* is a *Kālāteeta Purush,* a personality above Time.

25

Moksha: Salvation

Aims: Four Pursuits

The momentous life of Chānakya reminds us of some of his sayings that moulded his life and mind.

"The secret task of a king is to strive for the welfare of his people incessantly. The administration of the kingdom is his religious duty. His greatest gift would be to treat all as equals".

"The happiness of the commoners is the happiness of the king. Their welfare is his welfare. A king should never think of his personal interest or welfare, but should try to find his joy in the joy of his subjects."

After putting Chandragupta on the throne and making Mudrā Rākshasā as the Amātya, Chānakya devoted himself towards making the governance and the life of the people better. He truly followed the four pursuits of human life: Dharma, Artha, Kāma and Moksha. Kāma was only worry for him: incessant and diligently. Artha was needed only for living, not in cash but in kinds, utility goods which he got in abundance and felt no scarcity. He lived such a simple life that money became meaningless for him. It is a wonder that the person, who preached wealth and inspired others to be wealthy, had no wealth and actually, no need of wealth. He got Moksha, so he is a spirit now, a powerful spirit who adds values and power to an individual's spirit.

Activities after Retirement

After taking voluntary retirement, he wrote great works and penned in exquisite form his experiences in formula. That way he immortalized his wisdom for the posterity to use. On the one side he wrote freely and on the other kept sharp and agile eyes on the social and political functioning and developments of the nation that he had built up, and on his dear pupil for the sake of the dearest motherland.

It's evident from what is available that Chānakya had an intensely sharp and observant eyes along with a correlating and synthesizing mind who left nothing out of view and away from meaningful consideration. He had the opportunity to learn and see the turmoil, suffering, pain, luxury, loot, injustice, invasions, corruptions and everything else that was happening in closer vicinity and at a fair distance. Most of the time, he was himself in the firing line. He accumulated a wealth of theoretical and practical knowledge. It was overflowing. He knew that as Minister he could serve the living people but he won't be able to share his wealth. He decided to bring out that treasure and store in books for the posterity. For it he needed enough time, suitable and peaceful place and constant flow of current information. He made all necessary arrangements and one day he announced his voluntary retirement after appointing Amātya Rākshasā as the Prime Minister. All were shocked at it including the new Amātya who was expecting incessant interference by him.

None of them agreed to the proposal but it was Chānakya who was known for taking concrete decisions after a great deal of thinking over each pro and con. He succeeded in subsiding the temporary furore and retired for deep meditation and useful writing.

He happily and wisely spent his last days in active retirement.

After taking such voluntary retirement, he utilized his time in the best way possible under any circumstance. He did not break his relations with the vast kingdom that he had established rather he was deeply engaged in looking after it and strengthening it from outside with the help of his most efficient and active espionage system, that he had evolved, established and was running. He divided the rest of the time in two divisions: one for imparting training to administrators as the Āchārya; and the other in writing books. It was that period that he edited whatever he had written earlier and the new books that he wrote. In order to keep himself anonymous he wrote *Artha Shāstra* as **Kautilya;** *Kāma Sutra* as **Vātsyāyan;** and *Panchatantra* as **Vishnu Sharma,** which was his original name. He was the son of Rishi Chanak so, he was called Chānakya and as Chānakya he wrote *Chānakya Niti; Chānakya Sutra; Vriddha Chānakya.*

Organized Self

Chānakya was a well managed man that had control over the senses, and hence, over everything else. He laid down tough principles for the self and others; and he not only followed them sincerely and effortlessly but also forced others to follow them honestly and diligently. He enjoyed freedom and gave freedom but always in a disciplined and advantageous way. That is the reason that he never allowed the situations to slip away from his fingers, and the men to go beyond control. He maintained the discipline of the highest order.

Chānakya preferred physical health and good earning, not for sensuous pleasure but for refined sensibility and sublime soul. He says: As long as your body is healthy and under control and death is distant, try to save your soul; when death is imminent what can you do? So, it is always better to acquire as much knowledge as possible as wisdom gives everything desired and needed. In his words: Learning is like a cow of desire. It, like her, yields in all seasons. Like a mother, it feeds you on your journey. Therefore learning is a hidden treasure.

Chānakya had something to say about everything. Now, the things look traditional because of the long tradition of Chānakya himself but it is still as new and important as it was during his period. Take for example what he has to say about a son: A single son endowed with good qualities is far better than a hundred devoid of them. For the moon, though one, dispels the darkness, which the stars, though numerous, cannot. A stillborn son is superior to a foolish son endowed with a long life. The first causes grief for but a moment while the latter like a blazing fire consumes his parents in grief for life.

Chānakya has discussed at different places about self management which is an organized self; of time management by being friendly to time and by growing ability and skill so that a work can be completed well within the time schedule. He was conscious of the tiring body, fatigued mind and growing cost when a work takes more time, mostly because the person or persons concerned are not skilled. He has laid stress on the management of families, villages and organizations; and also the management of man, money and material.

Extreme Thinking: Balanced Life

He managed his time exquisitely well: perhaps counting and getting the maximum out of each precious minute. Such exquisite "time mangers" never fail. During the present time when quartz watches, showing correct time are available at each step: at walls, vehicles, wrists, mobiles etc, yet the flights are being delayed, cancelled, planes fall, communications fail, and late start of meetings, summits, international matches, live telecasts are forcing numerous men to wait or to return back in despair; that Chānakya set an example before all else to show "Hindu ways of management" that lays stress on growth from inside and on physical fitness and mental alertness.

Chānakya was a human being yet with his character, confidence, determination and wisdom, and of course, with his management skill and managerial insight and with an āchārya's knowledge and acumen, he controlled and forced the doom of King Mahānand. He judged the situation well and used the adverse events to the best of advantage. In the beginning, he seemed to be a loser, but soon he changed the tactics and started winning the frontiers kingdoms and isolated Nand dynasty from every side. Then the opponent had no option left but to surrender and it became easier for Chānakya to get control over the Magadha kingdom with ease as he was cut off from every side and could not get any help from outside. He was isolated and under check. Now, check and mate was the only possible result.

Chānakya got different unexpected rewards. That marks the success of the inner spirit, the success of Hindus way of meditation and spirituality, of inner growth and purity and sublimity. The Hindus sleep early, rise early, start early, and extend the working hours, and hence, enjoy leisure and get success. A grand success indeed! The whole world is afraid of the non-violent and peace loving Indians. And Indian students and employees are being attacked in every country despite the cry of globalization of almost everything.

Chānakya truly represents general pragmatic approach of the Indians on mass scale and of the spiritual and inner growth of the elite and shows all the credentials for which India is known: balance, sustenance, faith, hope and enlightenment. The way he analyses the situation in order to give fitting reply keeping in view all the segments as well as the whole, is typical Hindu synthesis, and moral approach to life.

What a balanced man was he! What an intellectual! What an intelligent figure that he had ready plans to reply so well! Once, he started getting success then there was nothing to stop him from achieving all. What a successful soul! The start may give an indication of success but it is the finish that actually decides success or failure! Follow Hindu way! Incessantly grow from inside! Remain fully alert and fresh and win the hurdles by sidelining the obstacles!

Chānakya had wider attitude and view that helped him in visualizing a United India and gave him immense success in actually uniting the whole country under one larger administration. Nowadays, people talk of globalization but are motivated and interested in petty gains for country's sake and for the sake of religion, region and race. Otherwise, in the wake of globalization there is no sense in talking and propagating racial culture and different religious concepts. During no other period in human history there were so many known and discussed castes, religion and religious views. Man is divided and become a very small unit with micro families and selfish philosophy. As a result people attack on the students, workers and other employees coming from other countries and states on racial grounds. Australian racial attacks on Indian students, is an eye-opener that the western people won't tolerate and digest greater inner growth and far superior performance from spiritually and morally rich and strong Indians. It is the degradation of man and totally non-effective and meaningless globalization.

There were no such petty feelings and jealous deeds during the time of Chānakya as the kings and ministers then ruled with iron rod, and of course, there was no politics of this lower order and there was no need to create and please vote-banks.

Everything to others

What a successful and fearless man was he! What a fearless daunty man! He moved in and out, up and down the whole kingdom without a guard of any sort and with a few books in his hand. What a sublime selfless service! He neither expected nor there were possibilities of gain. It was a grand example of Gitā's *nirlipta karma*, detached action, done without the expectation of a fruit. He turned his vow into reality in a very short span of time with very limited resources which he utilized patiently and fully. Chānakya kept nothing for himself. He gave every ounce of his knowledge, energy and ability to the people and nation. What a great sacrifice. He did not do adventurous deeds for personal pleasure, gain or accomplishment. He made Chandragupta the king and gave his own post to Mudrā Rākshasā, and lived a saintly life in seclusion yet remained active with his *guptachars* and timely advices. That is the greatest reason that he remained fearless but generated fear in others.

The Last Event

In the general planning of the book at least one event from the life of Chānakya has been presented at the beginning of each chapter, but for a change this event is being described at the close of the chapter and the book also; to show its importance and to announce another beginning which is always from an end. That is why the Time always joins the past and the future with the present. Time never separates. We wrongly declare that one is separated from one's near and dear ones. No, Time allows and gives opportunity to all, to get united with another and yet another. We are not separated from Chānakya. We are with him and he is in us with his teachings.

Death by Starvation

Chānakya kept on imparting the duties of the advisor of Bindusāra. Bindusāra had a minister named Subandhu who did not like Chānakya. One day, he told Bindusāra that Chānakya was responsible for the murder of his mother. Bindusāra asked the nurses who confirmed his story and he became very angry with Chānakya.

It is said that Chānakya, on hearing that the Emperor was angry with him, sent a piece of advice to the emperor telling him not to react and act without unveiling the real truth. Hearsay evidence is never enough.

Chānakya was now old and decided to die. There must have been Prayāshchit, atonement, behind his acceptance of death in prescribed manner but followed only by the Jains at that time. To die of starvation was his final decision. He declared and sat on a dung heap, ready to die by total abstinence from food and drink.

Meanwhile, Bindusāra checked the facts through one of the oldest maids alive. He heard the full story of his birth from that nurse. He realized that his mother was neither given poison nor took poison on her own, she had only shared meal with the king. He was angry with jealous Subandhu and beheaded him. He rushed to beg forgiveness of Chānakya. But Chānakya would not change his mind.

Bindusāra stayed there. His soldiers cleared the place cutting off the bushes etc. in no time. It was a clean place now. The news spread like wild fire. His disciples started coming but first to come were the villagers of that area. They came with the flowers and placed on the heap of the dung. It was covered by flowers. Chānakya sat "still" in meditation at the top in the centre among the flowers.

The Pandits chanted Veda Mantras and Mahāmritunaya Mantra. His pupils followed. Musicians played their instruments: drums, mridanga, Veenā, Sārangi, flutes and Shahnai as if it was an auspicious occasion. It was a rare sight. It was not death but pious and intentional departure from the world after completing all worldly duties. The purity of Chānakya's intention was projected. He departed, nay, he got Moksha, salvation.

Not only Bindusāra, the emperor but the people and pupils revered Chānakya and the loss of the greatest teacher and advisor was a considerable blow to them.

Appraisal

Deeds performed and wealth, prestige and legacy created make one's life meaningful. That life is no life which is spent in earning and accumulating wealth and spent in physical pleasure and luxurious living.

Effect

Our life must be useful for others and the final departure memorable.

BUSINESS
QUIZ BOOK

Author: Saurabh Aggarwal
Format: Paperback
Language: English
Page: 256
Price: ₹ 200
Publishers: V&S PUBLISHERS

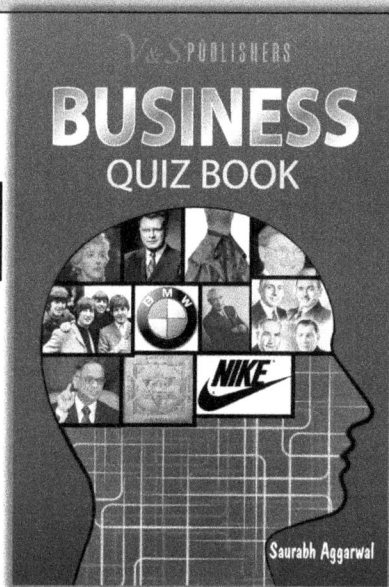

Did you know that crossword puzzles first appeared in the New York World in 1913, and soon became a popular feature in newspapers or that Kellog's as a brand had spent more than 100 years, $4000 on one page ad in the July issue of the Ladies Home Journal, Apple had lured John Sculley away from Pepsi because they wanted him to apply his marketing skills to the personal computer market. Find facts and trivia from the world of business that will amaze and delight you. The questions in this book have been framed in a way that they are: guessable with intelligent, lateral, or lucky thinking; interesting, amusing, or surprising; enjoyable, even to people who think they don't like quizzes; not so difficult that nobody knows the answer;

There are over 30 sections from automobiles, advertising, businessmen, FMCG to publications, management terms, quality control, management quotes. A special section for visual questions that are part of almost every business quiz these days has also been included.

The book will serve not just as a stepping stone for people who are interested in business quizzing but will prove to be an ideal compendium for all aspirants aiming for admission to professional colleges or career options in banking, insurance, defence, railways, state & central government services, besides many other top tier professions.

BEGINNERS' GUIDE TO
JOURNALISM
& MASS
COMMUNICATION

Author: Barun Roy
Format: Paperback
Language: English
Page: 124
Price: ₹ 150
Publishers: V&S PUBLISHERS

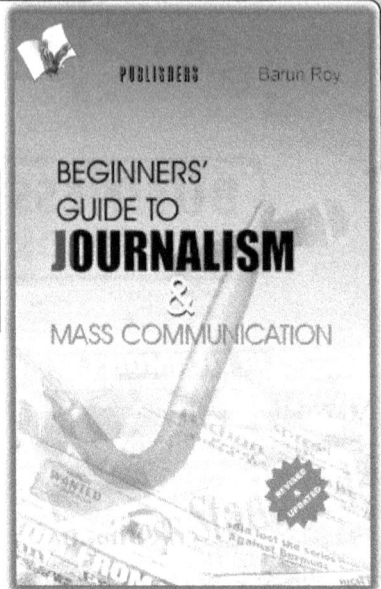

BEGINNERS'
GUIDE TO
JOURNALISM
&
MASS COMMUNICATION

Journalism today is an upcoming and a popular career offering bright prospects.

This book captures the scintillating thrill, sensational excitement, and vivacious action that is associated with journalism. The career-seekers find it difficult to gain the basic knowledge and the nitty-gritty of this highly electric and charged life. To fill in this void and fulfil the curiosity of such readers, this book has come up as a solution and has gained immense popularity solely because it is a comprehensive and impressive book dealing with all aspects of media.

It envelops all the facets and streams related to journalism in a succinct presentation. This book serves well the novices, students and practitioners alike and works as a fundamental, illuminative and informative text bearing all scholastic qualities.

Anyone interested in journalism, mass communication, media, advertising or public relations would find this book educative and helpful.

www.vspublishers.com • sales@vspublishers.com

Bestseller

Fix Your Problems
The Tenali Raman Way

FIX Your
PROBLEMS

The Tenali Raman's Way

Share his
Wits, Wisdom, Intellect and
Humour through
74 stories

Author: Vishal Goyal
Format: Paperback
Language: English
Page: 228
Price: ₹ 150
Publishers: V&S PUBLISHERS

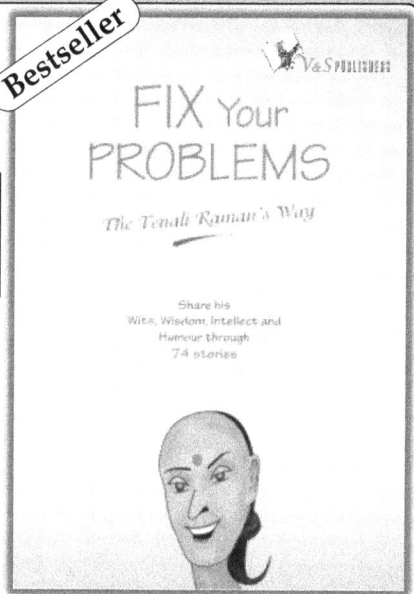

Tenali Raman was a court jester, an intelligent advisor and one of the *ashtadiggajas* (elephants serving as pillars and taking care of all the eight sides) in the Bhuvana Vijayam (Royal Court) of the famed Emperor of Vijayanagar Empire (City of Joy) in Karnataka– Sri Krishan Deva Raya (1509-1529), the moder ruler par excellence to Ashoka, Samudra Gupta and Harsha Vardhana. Tenali Raman was an embodiment of acute wit and humour and an admirable poet of knowledge, shrewdness and ingenuity. In a short span, the legacy left behind by Tenali Raman attained eternity. All these qualities of Tenali Raman have been fully explored and displayed in this collection of vibrant fables and anecdotes.

The book is a marvellous treasury of legends of Tenali Raman and Emperor Raya which evokes a long lost, never-never land: an enchanted world of alert wits and tricky gossips; crafty crooks with biting tongues, valiant brigands and an sssorted cluster of uncommon common people.

Narrated by the author and superbly illustrated, "Fix Your Problesm-The Tenali Raman Way" is an engaging blend of earthly wisdom and sparkling humour which deal with concepts that have certain timelessness. Each story is followed by terse moral and incalculable snippets which are usually that little extra that brings the reader a little more closer to his goal on the way to realisation.

www.ingramcontent.com/pod-product-compliance
Lightning Source LLC
Chambersburg PA
CBHW070405270326
41926CB00014B/2710